Understanding Autism
Spectrum Disorders

of related interest

Asperger Syndrome
A Guide for Parents and Professionals
Tony Attwood
ISBN 1 85302 577 1

Asperger Syndrome – What Teachers Need to Know
Matt Winter
Written for Cloud 9 Children's Foundation
ISBN 1 84310 143 2

How to Help a Clumsy Child
Strategies for Young Children with Developmental Motor Concerns
Lisa A. Kurtz
ISBN 1 84310 754 6

Parenting a Child with Asperger Syndrome
200 Tips and Strategies
Brenda Boyd
ISBN 184310 137 8

Snapshots of Autism
A Family Album
Jennifer Overton
ISBN 1 84310 723 6

Running with Walker
A Memoir
Robert Hughes
ISBN 1 84310 755 4

Understanding Autism Spectrum Disorders
Frequently Asked Questions

Diane Yapko

Jessica Kingsley Publishers
London and New York

First published in the United Kingdom in 2003
by Jessica Kingsley Publishers Ltd
116 Pentonville Road
London N1 9JB, England
and
29 West 35th Street, 10th fl.
New York, NY 10001-2299, USA

www.jkp.com

Copyright © Diane Yapko 2003

Library of Congress Cataloging in Publication Data
A CIP catalog record for this book is available from the Library of Congress

British Library Cataloguing in Publication Data
A CIP catalogue record for this book is available from the British Library

ISBN 1 84310 756 2

Printed and Bound in Great Britain by
Athenaeum Press, Gateshead, Tyne and Wear

To my husband Michael,
I dedicate this book to you with much love,
admiration, and respect for the life we have built
and shared together and all we have yet to build
in the future.

Contents

ACKNOWLEDGEMENTS   13

INTRODUCTION   17

Part 1: Diagnosis and Characteristics

1. What are Autism Spectrum Disorders (ASD)?   24

2. Is there a difference between High Functioning Autism and Asperger's Syndrome?   26

3. Are there medical tests to diagnose ASD?   28

4. How is ASD diagnosed?   29

5. What tests are used to diagnose ASD?   30

6. Who can diagnose ASD?   32

7. What are the common characteristics associated with a diagnosis of ASD?   34

8. At what age can ASD be diagnosed?   37

9. Are there gender differences in ASD?   39

10. How often does ASD occur? What is its prevalence?   39

11. Is there an ASD epidemic?   41

12. What conditions typically co-exist with ASD?   44

13. Can you cure ASD?   47

14. Are children with ASD mentally retarded?   47

15. What are the typical speech and language problems associated with ASD?   48

16. Are savant skills common in ASD?   52

17. What is Theory of Mind Deficit or Mindblindness?   52

18. What are Executive Function Deficits?   54

19. What are Central Coherence Deficits?   55

20. What are Nonverbal Learning Disabilities (NLD)?   56

21. What is Hyperlexia?   57

22. What is Pathological Demand Avoidance Sydrome (PDA)?   57

Part 2: Causes

23. What causes ASD?   63

24. Is ASD genetic?   65

25. Is there an ASD gene?   66

26. What are the chances of having more than one ASD child?   68

27. Can immunizations/vaccines cause ASD?   69

28. Can parenting style cause ASD?   70

29. Are there environmental causes of ASD?   71

30. Does a chemical imbalance in the brain cause ASD?   73

31. What medical conditions can cause ASD?   74

32. Can "Leaking" or "Leaky Gut" cause ASD?   75

33. What is the Opioid Excess Theory?   75

Part 3: Medical Issues

34. Can ASD be identified before birth?   79

35. Can ASD be identified at birth?   79

36. Are specific parts of the brain affected in ASD?   80

37. Is the immune system affected in ASD?   82

38. Is the gastrointestinal system affected in ASD?   83

39. What role do environmental toxins and viruses
    have in ASD?   84

40. What role do allergies play in children with ASD?   85

41. What is the "DAN" protocol?   86

42. What is "PANDAS"?   87

43. What are "Leaky Gut" and "Celiac Disease"?   88

44. What is Secretin?   89

45. Do all children with ASD have seizures?   91

46. How do I know if my child is having seizures?   92

47. What medications are used with ASD
    individuals?   94

48. What is Purine Autism?   95

49. What is the Urine Peptide Test?   96

Part 4: Treatments and Intervention Programs and Approaches

50. What types of treatment approaches exist for ASD?   100

51. Are all treatment approaches equally beneficial?   107

52. How do I decide which intervention(s) are most appropriate for my child?   109

53. What are Applied Behavioral Analysis (ABA) and Discrete Trial Training (DTT)?   112

54. What is Pivotal Response Training (PRT)?   114

55. What is Floor Time and the Developmental, Individual Difference, Relationship-based approach (DIR)?   115

56. What is the SCERTS Model?   116

57. What is TEACCH?   117

58. What is Speech-Language Therapy?   118

59. What is Augmentative Communication (AC) and PECS?   120

60. What is Auditory Integration Training (AIT)?   123

61. What is Occupational Therapy (OT)?   126

62. What is Sensory Integration Therapy (SI)?   127

63. What is Physical Therapy?   129

64. What is Art Therapy?   130

65. What is Animal Assisted Therapy?   130

66. What is Music Therapy?   131

67. What is Vision Therapy?   132

68. What diets are used to treat ASD individuals? 133

69. What vitamins and nutritional supplements
are used with ASD individuals? 135

70. What is Immunotherapy? 137

71. What medications are used to treat ASD? 137

72. How is Melatonin used in treating ASD? 139

73. Are there specific interventions for toilet
training? 139

74. Are there specific interventions for temper
tantrums? 140

75. Are there specific interventions for social skills
deficits? 141

76. Are there specific interventions for sleep
disturbances? 144

77. Are there specific interventions for self-injurious
behaviors? 146

78. Are there specific interventions for auditory
processing problems? 148

Part 5: Resources/Organizations/Websites

79. What organizations are available for ASD
individuals and their families? 153

80. What publications are available for ASD
individuals and their families? 157

81. What other resources, websites and books are available
for ASD individuals and their families? 163

82. What websites are available to provide therapy
tools, learning activities and materials for working
with ASD individuals? 197

Appendices

APPENDIX A DIAGNOSTIC CRITERIA FOR AUTISM   200

APPENDIX B DIAGNOSTIC CRITERIA FOR ASPERGER'S
            DISORDER   203

APPENDIX C DIAGNOSTIC CRITERIA FOR RETT'S
            DISORDER (DSM-IV, ICD-10 AND RETT
            SYNDROME ASSOCIATION)   206

APPENDIX D DIAGNOSTIC CRITERIA FOR
            CHILDHOOD DISINTEGRATIVE
            DISORDER   209

APPENDIX E TEST INSTRUMENTS   211

APPENDIX F MEDICATIONS   215

Acknowledgements

I have thought about writing this book for years, but finally making it happen is due to many different factors and people. Acknowledging them for their part in this process is a privilege.

First and foremost is my husband, Michael. I want to thank him on so many different levels. Having written over a dozen books and dozens of articles and book chapters himself, he is an incredible model from which to learn. His concentration, organizational skills, ability to structure himself, and his drive and determination to "work before play" are qualities I admire in him and strive to achieve. Without his constant encouragement, this book would not have happened. He was an active part from the beginning of this project to the end, from idea conception through thoughtful and helpful editing, to commiserating with me through some of my own frustrations. His ability to understand me, believe in me, support me, work with me, show pride in my strengths as well as tolerate my weaknesses, live with me and love me go beyond mere words of thanks. I will never have the ability to articulate to him what role he played in this project, but even more so in my life. I could never have done this book without you. Thank you, Michael, for everything you are and for everything you do. I love you.

I have been blessed with the best parents a person could hope for. They are loving, warm, caring, incredibly generous and fun people to be with. They are a constant source of inspiration for me. From the earliest times I can remember, my parents have continually supported me (and my brothers) in every endeavor, and encouraged me to do and be whatever I wanted. There was never external pressure to accomplish, yet they share pride in everything I do. Their love, support and encouragement is unwavering, unconditional and enduring. Your model as parents is unsurpassable and I respect you both for everything you have done and given of yourselves to fill that role so incredibly well. Thank you for providing me with the foundation for who I am today.

Having become so much a part of children's social skills and play development in my work, I have come to realize that my experience with my brothers, Kenny and Mitchell, was my first learning environment for developing my own play skills: how to join a game or invite someone to join, how to have conversations, how to understand humor and the differences between mean and fun teasing, and how to negotiate (although they may laugh and say I always got my way and therefore there really wasn't any negotiating). In addition to their own considerable professional accomplishments, both are loving husbands, fathers, and Kenny is even a grandfather. Thank you both for your love, support and enthusiasm. I also want to say how grateful I am to have your families in my life. Thanks to Sandi, David, Nicole, Catherine, Jackie, Nicole, Mike, Shawna, Brian and all their babies.

"Family" is a term that generates different meanings and feelings in people. For me, "family" has always been a foundation and source of unconditional love that, unlike a well, will never dry up. This project came too late to allow some beloved family members to share in its completion. Although they may not be here to see the book, they remain a part of it in my heart: my grandparents Sol and Betty Kemp, Mollie and Dave Cooper and my father-in-law, Benjamin Yapko. In addition to my biological family, my husband's family became mine 27 years ago and I thank Gerda and Brian Yapko for making me a part of their lives as if I were there from the start.

There is another family in my life, one I have chosen and love with all my heart: Wendy, Richard and Megan Horowitz. Richard and Wendy have been my best friends for almost 30 years, a special relationship that goes beyond words. Having given birth to Megan 12 years ago, they brought an incredible daughter into the world and especially into our lives. I treasure the day-to-day experiences we all share and I thank them for their love, support and laughter.

There have been many people whom I have had the privilege to learn from whom I have not previously had the chance to acknowledge for their role in my professional development. I have never forgotten the university professors or the colleagues from the Communicative Disorders Center at the University of California Medical Center, San Diego who played a significant role in my professional development. There are too many people to identify individually, but a few who I would like to mention here: Fran Austerlitz, Stephen Goldman, Carole Grote, Merle Irvin, Marilyn Newhoff, Edmond Thile, Doris Trauner and Beverly Wolfeck. A special thank you to Laura Schreibman for her time and editorial contributions to this book.

I am grateful to my publisher, Jessica Kingsley, for her willingness to take on this project. It is a tribute to their good communication, dedication and efficiency that Jessica and her staff have made this book possible.

Last, but not least, are the children and families I have worked with for 20 years who have touched me and motivated me to want to help them and to continue learning about the challenges associated with their special needs. Thank you for giving me the opportunity to be a part of your lives.

Diane Yapko, MA
Solana Beach, California

Introduction

Autism Spectrum Disorders (ASD) – a term not even in existence ten years ago – now has so much information available in the form of books, articles, websites, organizations, research studies and "experts" that it can be difficult to sort through and understand it all. That is why I wrote this book. I want to help readers get a brief overview of the extensive amount of information available, and have it all in one place in a simple, easy to use question and answer format.

There are many disciplines that address the issues associated with ASD and each one of them has enough information to fill several books in their own areas of expertise. There are researchers and there are clinicians, there are those interested in the cause and diagnosis and those interested in treatments, there are those interested in children and those interested in adults, and there are those who advocate legislation and those who provide information and support. ASD has many facets, and so do the various perspectives and biases that are presented in the scientific literature and popular media.

As a speech-language pathologist who has been in clinical practice working with children for over twenty years, and in giving workshops on the topic of Autism Spectrum Disorders to professionals and parents of children with ASD children, there are many questions that I am regularly asked to address.

This book provides answers to many of those common questions. Since the questions come primarily from individuals who do not have an expertise in ASD, their interest is usually in what will help a particular client or family member and to get clarification about some idea(s) they may have heard about in the media or from a family member or friend. So, while the science of ASD will be well represented here, some of the topics addressed in this book go beyond those advanced by the scientific community and include nontraditional treatments not currently supported by science but which I would be remiss to exclude here since they represent the current trends, terms and issues that are being discussed today among the teachers and parents with whom I consult.

This book is intended to provide the reader with the most current information available on common topics associated with ASD in the areas of diagnosis, causes, medical information, treatment and resources. Information is presented from a variety of perspectives in order to provide objective information to the reader. This book is likely to be most beneficial to individuals who are interested in learning about ASD without having to delve into the plethora of information that can be found in numerous resources. People who want quick and direct answers to specific questions will find this book a useful resource. People who want to know where to get more information on various aspects of ASD will find this book practical. People who want to understand some of the various terms or issues associated with ASD will find this book informative. Parents who have just had a child diagnosed with ASD will find this book supportive in its guidance.

I have tried to help the reader sort out which ideas are supported by scientific research and what is reported only anecdotally. Members of both the general lay public and professionals who have had success in using particular approaches in treatment become defensive when the scientific literature does not support their approach as efficacious. This does not mean the approach is not valid, but it does suggest caution is warranted so as not to elevate hope and have parents unrealistically try every new treatment someone happens to encourage. What works for one individual or family may or may not work for another. Whether an approach withstands scientific rigor is another issue altogether. Much to the dismay of the scientific and academic communities, most parents are simply interested in what has worked for others in order to know what might work for them. They are much less interested in whether the ideas have been supported by standards of science and peer reviewed in journals. Word-of-mouth is still the best advertising.

Given the range of possibilities, the purpose of this book is not to support any one perspective, idea or theoretical orientation. Rather, it is to expose you, the reader, to many of the current issues revolving around ASD and allow you to make up your own mind about the issues, pursue the avenues you wish, and be a critical thinker and consumer in obtaining information and support from professionals with experience in the area to guide you through the process. Toward that end, an extensive list of resources is provided in the last section of this book.

PART I

Diagnosis and Characteristics

1. What are Autism Spectrum Disorders (ASD)?

2. Is there a difference between High Functioning Autism and Asperger's Syndrome?

3. Are there medical tests to diagnose ASD?

4. How is ASD diagnosed?

5. What tests are used to diagnose ASD?

6. Who can diagnose ASD?

7. What are the common characteristics associated with a diagnosis of ASD?

8. At what age can ASD be diagnosed?

9. Are there gender differences in ASD?

10. How often does ASD occur? What is its prevalence?

11. Is there an ASD epidemic?

12. What conditions typically co-exist with ASD?

13. Can you cure ASD?

14. Are children with ASD mentally retarded?

15. What are the typical speech and language problems associated with ASD?

16. Are savant skills common in ASD?

17. What is Theory of Mind Deficit or Mindblindness?

18. What are Executive Function Deficits?

19. What are Central Coherence Deficits?

20. What are Nonverbal Learning Disabilities (NLD)?

21. What is Hyperlexia?

22. What is Pathological Demand Avoidance Syndrome (PDA)?

1 What are Autism Spectrum Disorders (ASD)?

Autism Spectrum Disorders (ASD) is a term used to describe a category of conditions also referred to as Pervasive Developmental Disorders (PDD). PDD includes: Autism or Autistic Disorder, Rett's Disorder, Childhood Disintegrative Disorder, Asperger's Disorder, and Pervasive Developmental Disorder–Not Otherwise Specified (PDD-NOS) which includes Atypical Autism. These disorders affect three primary areas of development: communication (verbal and nonverbal), social interaction and repetitive patterns of behavior, interest and activities. They have been grouped together under the single heading Pervasive Developmental Disorders in the Diagnostic and Statistical Manual of Mental Disorders (DSM-IV), the American Psychiatric Association's "bible" for diagnosing mental conditions. Another such manual for diagnosis used internationally, but less frequently in the United States, is the International Classification of Disease, 10th edition (ICD-10).

Autism or Autistic Disorder typically refers to the traditional or classical forms of what psychiatrist Leo Kanner identified in 1943 and labeled as "early infantile autism." According to the DSM-IV, a person must have 6 of the possible 12 diagnostic criteria in order to be given the diagnosis of Autism. At least two must be in the area of social impairments and at least one each in the areas of communication impairments and behavior/interests and activities. (See Appendix A for diagnostic criteria.) Most individuals with Autism have Mental Retardation.

Asperger's Disorder, also called Asperger's Syndrome, was initially described by Austrian physician Hans Asperger in Vienna in 1944. He identified children who had some similarities to those Kanner had described, but who also had some differences. Most notably these were the awkward use of language, the lack of humor and the strange use of nonverbal communication including eye contact, gestures, posture, and inflection patterns (prosody). For reasons that are not known, Asperger's work was not widely publicized in English-speaking countries until Lorna Wing wrote about his work in the 1980s. It was not until the mid 1990s that the label was included in the diagnostic manuals (DSM-IV and ICD-10). There are eight diagnostic criteria for Asperger's Syndrome. Of these, a person must have at least two impairments in social interaction and at least one in behavior/interest and activities. Unlike a diagnosis of Autism, in Asperger's Syndrome, current diagnostic criteria indicate there are no clinical significant delays in either language or cognitive development (see Appendix B for diagnostic criteria for Asperger's Syndrome).

Rett's Disorder (or Rett Syndrome) is characterized by the loss of previously acquired skills and the development of a frequent hand-wringing behavior. There is a deceleration of head growth between 5 and 48 months, severely impaired expressive and receptive language with severe psychomotor retardation, and a loss of social engagement, which often develops again after the preschool years. Rett Syndrome is usually associated with severe or profound Mental Retardation. Unlike the other ASDs, Rett Syndrome primarily affects females and a specific gene mutation (MECP2) has been associated with the diagnosis. Not all individuals with Rett Syndrome have an identifiable mutation in MECP2 and not all individuals with a MECP2 mutation have Rett Syndrome. (See Appendix C for a description of Rett Syndrome diagnostic criteria.)

Childhood Disintegrative Disorder is characterized by a period of normal development for at least the first two years and then a loss of previously acquired skills before the age of ten. The loss of skills occurs in at least two of the following areas: language, social, adaptive skills, bowel or bladder control, play and motor skills (see Appendix D for diagnostic criteria for Childhood Disintegrative Disorder).

Pervasive Developmental Disorder–Not Otherwise Specified (PDD-NOS) is the ASD label used when a person exhibits impairments in the social interaction, communication (verbal and nonverbal) and stereotyped behaviors, interests and activities but they do not meet the criteria set forth in the diagnosis of Autism or the other PDD labels. Essentially, PDD-NOS is used for a person whose behaviors and abilities are described as "Autistic-like" but do not meet enough (6 out of the 12 criteria) or are not severe or significant enough to warrant the diagnosis of Autism.

Many people believe that the term PDD is too general and has not adequately addressed the diversity of conditions associated with this label. With the evolution of newer classification systems, such as multi-system neurological disorders and regulatory disorders, many of the current terms may eventually be replaced.

2 Is there a difference between High Functioning Autism and Asperger's Syndrome?

Yes and no depending upon who you ask. Even the term "High Functioning" Autism is somewhat ambiguous since it refers to an individual who has more functional skills than another individual diagnosed with "just" Autism. There is agreement that Autism runs on a continuum from mild to severe, but there is no clear delineation between a mildly impaired or high functioning individual and a moderately or severely impaired individual. These are terms used to help individuals clarify differences in ability or functional level, but their use is not consistent between professionals or the general public.

There are criteria in the DSM-IV, as described in the previous question and noted in Appendix B, that differentiate Autism from Asperger's Syndrome (AS), but where on the Autism continuum AS may merge, or whether it is a separate diagnostic entity from High Functioning Autism continues to be debated today. Asperger himself did not list specific criteria for inclusion in such a diagnosis, but subsequent researchers have chosen their own, different, criteria when studying individuals with Asperger's Syndrome. This has led to much confusion in the research.

At the time of writing the answer that best addresses this question is to distinguish the terms according to why they are used. If one is using the term in research to help in identifying similarities and differences in specific genetic markers, brain neurochemistry, or structure, behaviors and abilities, then it may be that there is a distinction between High Functioning Autism and Asperger's Syndrome. But if the term is being used to identify an individual for treatment (clinically, educationally, etc), then the difference at this point in time is irrelevant. The treatment approaches and strategies that are used for individuals with High Functioning Autism are the same as those used for individuals with Asperger's Syndrome. That is not to say that each individual, regardless of their diagnostic label, requires an individualized approach to treatment – certainly from individual to individual there will be differences – but there is no clinically significant difference in these groups when dealing with and treating the day-to-day issues that present themselves.

3 Are there medical tests to diagnose ASD?

No. There are now many new studies looking at ways to diagnose ASD medically, but currently there are no medical tests, no genetic markers, no blood tests or brain scans that can diagnose ASD.

Medical tests are often ordered when a person is being evaluated for ASD, but this is to either rule in or out other medical conditions rather than confirm a diagnosis of ASD. Some of the tests which a physician may order include:

- a hearing test which may include an audiogram, tympanogram and brain stem auditory evoked response test (BAER) which are used to determine whether there is a hearing impairment

- chromosome or DNA testing to consider the diagnosis of Fragile X Syndrome or other chromosomal or gene abnormalities

- chemical and metabolic studies to look at various conditions for which special diets may be warranted

- brain scans (e.g., CT scan, MRI) to look for neurological conditions, tumors, or to rule out Tuberous Sclerosis

- EEGs which measure brain waves to consider a seizure disorder or Landau-Kleffner Syndrome.

There is promising new research now being conducted which may help in the identification and subsequent prevention and treatment of ASD. Studies funded by a coordinated group of organizations led by head researcher Dr Karin Nelson[1] of the National Institute of Neurological Disorders and Stroke (NINDS) is identifying brain proteins which are crucial in the development of the nervous system and which may help to identify Autism and Mental Retardation at birth.

From the Human Genome Project, we have learned that there are susceptible spots on some chromosomes (2, 6, 7, 15, 16, 17), but at this time they do not predict or confirm a diagnosis of ASD.

The only way to diagnose ASD at present is with a combination of observation and questions, ideally from a multidisciplinary team of professionals with experience in ASD (as described in the next question).

4 How is ASD diagnosed?

A diagnosis of ASD is made from a comprehensive assessment of both historical information and current abilities. Areas addressed in a comprehensive assessment often require a multidisciplinary team of professionals who can each address specific aspects of development. Who does such an assessment is addressed in question 6 in this section.

As indicated previously, there are currently no medical tests available which can diagnose ASD. The diagnosis is made from a combination of observations, questionnaires and standard-

---

1   For more information on the study conducted by Dr Karin Nelson, contact the March of Dimes-California Birth Defects Monitoring Program on (00 1) 888-898-2229 (in the United States) or at www.cbdmp.org.

ized tests (listed in question 5 and further described in Appendix E), which measure various aspects of behavior and ability in several different areas of development. In order to make a diagnosis of ASD, a person must meet certain criteria that are listed in the diagnostic manuals referred to as DSM-IV-R or ICD-10. These manuals are used by health professionals to diagnose most conditions and the criteria for diagnosing ASD are listed in Appendices A–D.

Unlike a blood test in which you can objectively identify something that is, or is not, present in the blood, observations and questionnaires are a far more subjective means of assessment. That is one reason why individuals may have difficulty obtaining an accurate diagnosis. Asking a parent about a child's behavior is not exactly "scientific." Deciding whether a child's behavior is "normal" or "average" for their age or "unusual" requires sophisticated observational skills and references for what is "normal" or "average" or "unusual." In addition, parents are often asked to report on how their child behaved many years earlier, and this can be quite difficult since recall can be distorted by the passage of time.

5 What tests are used to diagnose ASD?

There are a number of standardized tests and questionnaires used by various professionals to assist in the diagnosis of ASD. In order to determine whether an individual meets the criteria of DSM-IV or ICD-10, professionals may use Autism checklists, clinical observations and/or direct questions. In addition, diagnosis may include more extensive testing in a number of deficit areas, such as speech and language problems, sensory and motor problems, as well as attention, learning and cognitive deficits.

There are many different questionnaires/rating scales designed specifically to screen and diagnose ASD, and more tools are being developed and researched at this time. Some of these instruments are listed below. (This list is by no means exhaustive.) Additional information on each of the tests is available in Appendix E.

- Asperger Syndrome Diagnostic Scale (ASDS)
- Autism Behavior Checklist (ABC)
- Autism Diagnostic Interview–Revised (ADI-R)
- Autism Research Institute (ARI) Form E-2: Diagnostic Checklist
- Autism Screening Instrument for Educational Planning (ASIEP-2)
- Behavior Observation Scale for Autism (BOS)
- Behavior Rating Instrument for Autistic and Other Atypical Children (BRIAC)
- Childhood Autism Rating Scale (CARS)
- Gilliam Asperger's Disorder Scale (GADS)
- Gilliam Autism Rating Scale (GARS)
- Pervasive Developmental Disorders Screening Test (PDDST)
- Pre-linguistic Autism Diagnostic Observation Schedule (PL-ADOS)
- Screening Test for Autism in Two-Year-Olds
- The Australian Scale for Asperger's Syndrome
- The Modified Checklist for Autism in Toddlers (M-CHAT).

The standardized tests which are used to evaluate speech, language, pragmatics, hearing/processing, motor skills, sensory integration, cognitive abilities, attention, learning and behavior are quite large in number and beyond the scope of this book to list.

6   Who can diagnose ASD?

There is no single individual who is fully responsible for the diagnosis of ASD. There are a number of individuals who can be involved in a diagnosis of ASD. Depending upon whether you work through the medical system or the educational system, different people may be involved in formulating a diagnosis.

Often, parents will contact their physician first when they are concerned about their child's development. It may be the physician who first suspects the diagnosis, but often pediatricians are not trained in such specialty areas and do not typically have the time in an office visit to obtain the necessary history, make necessary observations and get answers to the many questions that are necessary for a diagnosis. More often, a pediatrician will refer you to a specialist in the area of ASD or the area of concern. For example, if the concern is that your child is behaviorally difficult to manage (e.g., temper tantrums; difficult to console; rigid, repetitive patterns of behaviors), your physician may refer you to a psychologist or behavior specialist for an evaluation, and he or she may be the one to make the diagnosis. Or, if the concern is that your child is not properly developing speech and language or has lost skills in those areas, your physician may refer you to a speech-language pathologist who may make the diagnosis.

WHO Evaluates?	WHAT is evaluated?
Physician	Medical status: general health and history, medications. Primary referral source to specialists.
Neurologist	Specialty physician assesses neurological status and may order EEG, CT or MRI scans, metabolic and chemical workups.
Psychologist	Developmental and emotional status, cognitive abilities, psychometric tests, achievement tests, social skills, attention and behavior.
Behavior Specialist or Autism Specialist	Usually a psychologist who specializes in assessing and providing treatment recommendations related to behavioral issues.
Speech-Language Pathologist	Speech/articulation/oral-motor abilities, receptive and expressive language, nonverbal language (including potential for sign or augmentative communication), pragmatic language, social skills, attention, processing and behavior.
Audiologist	Hearing (air/bone conduction, middle ear functioning), Central Auditory Processing, attention and behavior.
Occupational Therapist	Fine motor abilities, sensory integration skills, attention and behavior.
Physical Therapist	Gross motor abilities, strength and range of movement, attention and behavior.
Social Worker or Public Agency Case Worker	Historical information gathered, general development, support service availability and eligibility.
Classroom Teacher, Resource Specialist and/or Special Education Teacher	Overall ability to function within the classroom including observation of academic, social, motor, attention and behavior. Standardized tests in achievement include: reading, writing, math, etc.

If your first contact is with the educational system, then typically a team of individuals become involved in a multidisciplinary assessment of your child. This team usually includes a psychologist, speech-language pathologist, occupational therapist, physical therapist, teacher and school administrator. Depending upon what country you live in, laws and guidelines are different for who is involved in the diagnosis of ASD.

A quick overview of possible professionals involved in the evaluation process is provided in the table on the previous page.

7 What are the common characteristics associated with a diagnosis of ASD?

Each child can manifest symptoms of his or her ASD in different ways and in varying degrees of severity from mild to severe. A basic premise is that the deficits are "distinctly deviant relative to the individual's developmental level or mental age" (DSM-IV, 1994) and occur prior to the age of three.

There have traditionally been three areas of development which are affected in individuals with ASD: communication, social interaction and behavior. However, the characteristics associated with each of the current diagnostic labels vary. For example, with a diagnosis of Autism, a child's speech may not develop at all or may develop and then be lost (as in Rett Syndrome), whereas a diagnosis of Asperger's Syndrome assumes adequate speech development. Several characteristics can fall into more than one category. For example, difficulty with understanding and using humor is related to both communication and social deficits. Some other characteristics, such as sensory integrative dysfunction, do not easily fit into the existing triad of communication, social interaction and behavior but affect all three areas. Additionally, a diagnosis of Autism often has mental retardation as a characteristic while a diagnosis of AS suggests no such cognitive impairment. Despite these difficulties with categorization, a list of key characteristics of ASDs is listed below. Not all individuals have all of these characteristics and the symptoms range on a continuum from mild to profound, thus resulting in a very heterogeneous (diverse) group of individuals.

Communication

- Delay or lack of speech and language development.
- Loss of speech development previously demonstrated.
- Poor or limited expressive or receptive language skills.
- Apparently adequate speech and language but poor or no ability to engage in sustained conversation.
- Repetitive, stereotyped or idiosyncratic use of language (jargon) – individuals who use the same word/phrases/topics over and over again; those who repeat phrases from commercials/books/ videos and make up their own language and way of using it with others.
- Echolalia – the repetition of what someone else has said either immediately after them (immediate echolalia) or after a period of time (delayed echolalia).
- Monotone or limited variability in vocal inflection.

- Poor or limited nonverbal communication (e.g., pointing, gesturing).

- Poor or limited understanding of language beyond its concrete meaning (e.g., difficulty with humor, figurative language, metaphor).

Social Interaction

- Peer social interaction can range from totally absent to inability to maintain desired relationships.

- Limited to no development of pretend or imaginative play.

- Limited development in the typical expansion upon play themes.

- Limited to no symbolic use of toys.

- Rote, repetitive, rigid and inflexible in play and games.

- Poor to limited understanding and use of nonverbal behaviors (e.g., eye contact, facial expression, postures and gesturing) to regulate social interaction.

- Lack of, or limited social reciprocity (the give and take of a social exchange).

- Sensory impairments (e.g., auditory, tactile) that interfere with the ability to respond and participate in social exchanges and play.

Behavior

- Preoccupation with certain areas of interest and parts of objects.

- Self-stimulating behaviors may be verbal (repeating sounds/phrases) or motoric (rocking, spinning, pacing, hand flapping).

- Rigid adherence to routines and rituals, often nonfunctional in nature and idiosyncratic.

- Difficulty with play skills including limited to no imagination or symbolic play, rigid and routinized play schemes, routines and rituals.

- Repetitive motor movements (e.g., hand flapping, twirling, complex body movements).

- Rigid and repetitive patterns of behavior, interest and activities.

8 At what age can ASD be diagnosed?

ASD is a diagnosis that can be obtained at any time during a lifespan, but the symptoms that characterize the disorders must be present prior to the age of three. Some of the behaviors associated with ASD can be observed as early as in infancy. For example, parents report that their infants were not responsive to them, didn't look at them, or thwarted being held, that they cried inconsolably, and that they didn't appear to hear or did not alert to various sounds. Although in hindsight (once a child has been diagnosed) these behaviors may seem "obvious" to the diagnosis of ASD, at the time of their first observation the behaviors are often attributed to other, more benign reasons (such as just being a colicky baby).

There are currently studies underway looking at the attention and social behaviors of children during their first year of life. Early results suggest that certain observations can be made in whether a child attends to social or nonsocial stimuli, which may lead to early diagnosis of ASD in the future. Research in this area is in the very earliest stages.

It is especially difficult for first time parents to notice deviancies in a child's development because they may not have the knowledge or reference points for what is considered "normal." This brings up a very critical issue regarding the age of diagnosis for ASD since qualitative behaviors need to be significantly and markedly different from "normal" for the child's age. When a child is only six months old, there is not a lot of room for "difference from normal." Additionally, there is great variability in "normal" acquisition of developmental milestones such as when a child first uses speech or begins to walk. Therefore, it is rare that a child would currently be diagnosed with ASD prior to the age of 12 months when critical developmental milestones are still expected to emerge, and then only by a professional with extensive experience with young ASD children. It is more common that a diagnosis would be given around two or three years of age. However, the subtler or less severe the characteristics, the harder it is to make a diagnosis at a young age.

ASD is not just diagnosed during childhood. In fact, many adults are now being diagnosed as ASD: people for whom no such category label existed when they were growing up. These individuals may have previously been labeled mentally retarded, learning disabled, attention deficit disordered, emotionally disturbed or just odd or eccentric. Adults seeking a diagnosis will need to rely upon historical records and reports to help make the diagnosis since the criterion for the diagnosis is an age of onset prior to the age of three.

9 Are there gender differences in ASD?

Yes, but they change depending upon which of the Autism Spectrum Disorders is being examined. When Kanner initially identified Autism, he identified four times as many boys as girls affected with Autistic Syndrome. That difference has essentially remained the same with the 1994 DSM-IV report of a four to five times higher rate of Autism in males than in females. As classification labels blur and more studies are conducted, the rates may not be as high as initially or currently reported, although males do continue to significantly outnumber females. When females are diagnosed with Autism, they are typically more severely affected and exhibit more severe mental retardation.

Rett Syndrome affects primarily females for reasons that are not clear. Rett Syndrome is considered to be much less common than Autism.

In Childhood Disintegrative Disorder, which is considered quite rare, studies initially suggested an equal number of boys and girls affected. More current studies indicate that it may be more common among males.

Asperger's Syndrome is considered to be more common in males although specific data are limited since this diagnostic term has only recently been included in DSM-IV.

10 How often does ASD occur? What is its prevalence?

Autism Spectrum Disorders vary in their prevalence, or how often they occur. In addition, with the broader category labels and more recent research, prevalence data are changing. In fact, the number of individuals diagnosed with ASD is rising dramatically and has raised the question of whether there is an epidemic. This issue is addressed in question 11.

Depending upon which literature you read, you will get different prevalence data. The older data represent ASD as a relatively rare developmental disorder, while the newer research suggests it is much more common than previously realized.

According to the Diagnostic and Statistical Manual–4th edition (DSM-IV), only Autistic Disorder has a number of cases associated with it while the other diagnostic labels within the ASD category instead have a narrative description of their prevalence. The following prevalence data are reported:

- Autistic Disorder: 2–5 per 10,000

- Rett's Disorder: "much less common than Autistic Disorder"

- Childhood Disintegrative Disorder: "very rare and much less common than Autistic Disorder"

- Asperger's Disorder: Prevalence data is limited

- PDD-NOS: Not addressed in the DSM-IV.

According to more recent studies, presented at the International Meeting for Autism Research conference held in San Diego in November 2001, Autism may be as high as 68 per 10,000 or 1 in every 147 individuals. Some research suggests that there are hundreds of thousands of individuals with PDD-NOS or atypical PDD who are undiagnosed.

11   Is there an ASD epidemic?

Many researchers and professional organizations have identified an increase in the number of people diagnosed with ASD over the past decade. At the time of writing, new statistics were being provided almost daily for different regions of the world showing an increase in the diagnosis of Autism Spectrum Disorders. In fact, certain pockets or population areas have had a significant increase relative to the general population and this fact, along with other data, has raised the question of whether there is an ASD epidemic.

Eric Fombonne's work, presented in November 2001 at the International Meeting for Autism Research, suggests that the rates of Autism in the last 25 years have increased anywhere from 600% to 3400% depending upon which criteria are used. If data are considered in the middle of this range, it suggests that Autism has risen 1300% over the past quarter century. Another way of looking at these data is to think of Autism rates doubling every two years between 1976 and 2001.

Why the increase? The answer is not clear. Certainly, there is a much greater awareness of and ability to diagnose the disorder. Additionally, when the diagnostic criteria are expanded to include higher functioning children with Asperger's Syndrome and PDD-NOS, one would expect larger numbers. But a recent study in California (2002) suggests that these reasons alone do not account for some of the very alarming statistics. Something else seems to be going on, but no one is sure what. Research is being undertaken around the world to determine why such an increase in ASD has been occurring.

Prevalence data are not available from all countries, nor are the ways of documenting the disorder consistent, but a few countries are provided below to give the reader a sense of the marked increase in this diagnosis worldwide.

United States

A 1999 report by the California Department of Developmental Services (DDS), which operates the developmental regional centers, found a 273% increase in Autism cases between 1987 and 1998. The report was the catalyst for funding a $1 million appropriation to identify the factors responsible for the increase.

The DDS reported that 37% of all new intakes are accounted for by the diagnosis of Autism (not including PDD-NOS, Asperger's Syndrome or any other ASD). The most recent numbers indicate a rate of nine children per day, seven days a week, qualifying for services in California. In the first quarter of 2002, there were 812 new cases of Autism added to California's developmental services system, which is a record. In 2001 the first six months saw more children added to the California system than in any other full year between 1969 and 1998. It is estimated that California will add over 2700 new children with Autism to its system, which is equal to the number of children added in the 13.5 years prior to 1979/1980.

In a study by the Center for Disease Control (CDC), there are pockets of increased incidence such as in Brick Township, New Jersey, where the reports include:

- 4 in 1000 children diagnosed with Autism

- 6.7 in 1000 children diagnosed with Asperger's or PDD-NOS

- 23 studies pre-1998 indicated prevalence 0.19 to 2.11 per 1000

- 3 studies after 1998 listed prevalence between 3.08 to 6.0 per 1000.

United Kingdom

Some studies in England suggest there is a sevenfold increase in the number of new cases of Autism between 1983 and 1999. A study by the Autism Research Centre at Cambridge University suggested a possible rate of 1 in every 175 primary school aged children.

In a study by Chakrabarti and Fombonne, reported in the *Journal of the American Medical Association* (June 2001), the prevalence of PDD in preschool children in the Staffordshire region of the UK was estimated to be 62.6 children per 10,000. Another study at the Autism Research Centre at Cambridge University reported the prevalence of ASD in 5–11-year-olds to be 57 in 10,000.

Ireland

The Irish Society for Autism reported an increase in their rates of Autism from 5 per 10,000 in 1996 to 15 in 10,000 in 2002.

Iceland

In individuals born between 1974 and 1983 the rate of Autism was 4.8 per 10,000, while in those born between 1984 and 1993 the rate increased to 8.6 per 10,000.

Japan

In the 1980s prevalence rates were 5–16 per 10,000, while in 1996 it was 21.1 per 10,000.

12   What conditions typically co-exist with ASD?

There are a number of different conditions that can occur along with a diagnosis of Autism Spectrum Disorder. These are referred to as "co-existing" conditions.

Mental Retardation

Mental Retardation usually accompanies the diagnosis of ASD with the exception of Asperger's Syndrome in which there is no clinically significant delay in cognitive functioning. Mental Retardation is a term used to define a population based upon a score usually obtained on intelligence tests. Individuals can obtain scores that yield mild, moderate or severe mental retardation.

Seizure Disorder

Abnormal EEG findings with, or without, a Seizure Disorder is also commonly seen in individuals diagnosed with ASD. For some individuals this may not appear until adolescence.

Attention Deficit Disorders (ADD, ADHD)

Attention Deficit Disorders are a separate diagnostic category from ASD, although attentional issues are certainly part of the ASD profile. A person can be diagnosed with ASD and also an Attention Deficit Disorder or the attentional factors may simply be part of the ASD and not meet the criteria for a separate diagnosis. Attention Deficit Disorders include difficulties with focused attention, distraction and impulsivity. Most individuals with ASD have difficulty focusing on tasks, are often easily distracted by either external stimuli (such as things they see or hear) or by internal stimuli (their own thoughts, TV or movie scenes, etc). The diagnosis of Attention Deficit Hyperactivity Disorder (ADHD) is given when an individual also experiences an increase in activity level compared to age matched peers. Many parents will identify with the hyperactivity of the children with ASD, who can't seem to sit still, are constantly moving even when they are seated, climb furniture, walls and anything else they can ascend.

Obsessive-Compulsive Disorder (OCD)

Whether OCD is a separate condition from or part of the diagnosis of ASD continues to be debated. Again, it is a separate diagnostic label and individuals can have ASD, OCD or both. Obsessions refer to thoughts, whereas compulsions refer to behaviors. Individuals with ASD often engage in various repetitive and ritualistic behaviors. Whether it is the wringing or flapping of hands, self-stimulating spinning or the lining up of items, these behaviors are referred to as compulsive behaviors. It is not known if they occur for the same reason as other compulsive behaviors, such as having to wash one's hands over and over again or checking more than once to see if the door is locked, which are typically seen in individuals with OCD.

Obsessive thoughts can only be inferred from the behavior or repetitive verbalizations of lower functioning individuals. However, with individuals who are functioning at the higher end of the spectrum, obsessive thoughts can monopolize their conversations.

Auditory Processing Disorders

It is common that individuals with ASD also have auditory processing problems. But auditory processing problems are also seen in individuals without ASD. Most common in the ASD population is the delayed maturation of the central auditory pathways and the difficulties in integrating information between the right and left hemisphere. Additionally, one of the most common auditory processing problems observed in this group of individuals is their difficulty in listening to auditory information in the presence of background noise or competing auditory information.

Sensory Integration Disorders

Individuals with ASD often have co-morbid Sensory Integration Disorders. They have difficulty in appreciating spatial issues (e.g., their own body in space or in relation to objects or people), balance, and getting the appropriate neurological feedback from the senses in order to regulate their body and perceptions. Getting the two hemispheres of the brain to work together along with correctly perceiving and acting upon the input the brain receives from the senses is an area of difficulty for many individuals with ASD.

Tourette's Syndrome

Tourette's Syndrome is a disorder characterized by involuntary disturbances called tics. There are different kinds of tics. They can be vocal (e.g., grunting, throat clearing, barking sounds or verbalizations) or motor (e.g., jerking movements of the head or other body parts, facial twitching or eye blinking). Tics are often part of Autism and recognizing whether the behaviors are distinct from the ASD label often takes much observation and experience. Although there is some evidence to suggest that Tourette's is a co-existing condition with ASD, there has also been evidence of the higher incidence of Tourette's with OCD, ADHD and Bipolar Disorder. Research continues in this area.

The specific deficit areas will need to be addressed regardless of whether these disorders are part of the ASD profile or separate diagnoses co-existing with ASD.

13   Can you cure ASD?

No. With our current knowledge of ASD, there is not a "cure" per se. However, there is evidence that individuals who receive appropriate, early and intensive intervention have made considerable gains. Some have improved from initially severely impaired to moderately or even mildly impaired. How severe an individual "looks" depends upon age and the expectations placed upon them for the context in which they are functioning.

In the 1960s psychologist Ivar Lovaas used behavioral approaches to treat Autistic children. He claimed he cured them with this approach. Although he provided a program that allowed these children to make substantial progress, the claim of having cured anyone is suspect. Subsequent studies have not replicated his findings. However, support for behavioral interventions is strong and may be quite helpful for many in this population.

While there are isolated stories of individual parents who claim to have "cured" their child with a particular approach, all scientific evidence indicates there is currently no "cure" for Autism. Many different therapeutic interventions can and do reduce or even eliminate some or many of the specific symptoms associated with Autism, but none provide a full cure. Early intervention remains the best treatment for helping a child improve.

14   Are children with ASD mentally retarded?

Most children (between 50–75%) with ASD fall in the range of mentally retarded on standardized intelligence tests. This usually means their intelligence quotient (IQ) is below the average range and that number varies depending upon which tests are used to measure intelligence. Most often, intelligence tests use a scale with 100 being considered the average plus or minus 15 points. Those individuals whose IQ is 85 to 70 are considered below average while those whose score is below 70 are typically referred to as mentally retarded.

It is important to note that these intelligence tests are difficult for ASD individuals to take and may not adequately demonstrate much of their true intelligence because of the heavy emphasis on language. That is not to say that if all the language aspects were pulled out of the tests (as they are in some tests) that these individuals would be considered to be of average intelligence. But, it is important to note when using standardized instruments to measure a child's intelligence that a child with ASD may or may not do well on such tests depending upon their specific deficits.

15   What are the typical speech and language problems associated with ASD?

Before describing the problems typically seen in children with ASD, it might be helpful to have a brief description of what is considered "normal" or "typical" early speech and language development. Children begin making sounds as an infant. They produce vowel sounds called cooing. Usually this is produced as a prolonged vowel sound such as "aaaaaaaaa" or "uuuuuuuu." Around six months, they begin to add consonants to their repertoire and begin the process called "babbling" (e.g., ba-ba-ba, ma-ma-ma, ga-ga-ga). Shortly thereafter, the inflections of "normal speech" without the real words begin to emerge "as if" the child is talking. Usually, by the time a child reaches his/her first birthday, they have begun to produce single meaningful words (e.g., more, juice, car, ball). Speech continues to progress rapidly from this point as single words begin to be produced next to each other and then combine into true two word phrases (e.g., my book, no bed, go park, more slide). By the age of three, simple sentences are used to communicate a wealth of information and include a number of linguistic concepts, although not all grammatical concepts are used, or used correctly.

Speech and language development relates not just to the sounds or words spoken (called "expressive abilities") but also to the understanding of that language (called "receptive abilities"). Children by the age of two are following most simple two-step directions ("get the ball, give it to daddy;" "put the cup in the sink"). These directions contain various concepts that are understood at this young age including prepositions (spatial words such as on, in, up, down), quantity concepts (one, more, all); pronouns (mine, yours) and a number of other linguistic concepts.

A child's ability to engage with the adult world is not solely based upon verbal abilities. Under a year old, a child's gaze can direct a communication, their turn-taking skills with an adult are developing, and their ability to point is a significant and important stage in the development of shared attention and communication. A child's language, even at the one word stage at approximately a year, can have various intentions. They are able to request (juice, more, ball); negate (no, stop); question (dat? for "what's that?"); and various other functions. These developmental milestones have some variability to them, but in general, by the age of two, most children are speaking in simple two–three word sentences, following simple directions and communicating often with the people in their environment.

The types of speech and language problems that can be seen in the ASD population can vary significantly. Some children appear to develop "normally" for the first 18–24 months following the developing milestones described above and then lose their skills. This is called a regression in abilities. Others start to develop the early milestones such as cooing and babbling and then stop in their development. Still others experience speech and language problems from the start as the developmental milestones described above never appear. About half of Autistic individuals remain mute their whole lives. Some who do not speak can develop the ability to communicate through pictures or other augmentative systems, but some do not. Some individuals are delayed in their developmental milestones: they go through them at a much slower rate and do not develop words or simple sentences until they are seven or eight years old. This is not typical, and the longer a child goes in his or her development without speech, the greater the likelihood that they will not develop speech.

Some individuals develop a type of speech referred to as "echolalia." This is where the child repeats or parrots back what has been said, sometimes immediately, and sometimes hours or days later. Words and phrases from one context can be produced at a later time in an apparently unrelated context. Some children develop the ability to parrot phrases and inflectional patterns from TV characters, commercials, and movies but do not develop more meaningful or traditional ways of communicating.

Auditory processing and language processing difficulties are observed in most individuals with ASD and these include problems with auditory attention, discrimination of sounds/words, auditory memory, auditory synthesis or blending and auditory figure-ground tasks (differentiating the important signal from background noise).

Many individuals with ASD have difficulty understanding and using pronouns. Words like "me," "my," "you," and "your" can cause confusion. This is due to the difficulty in understanding how the word's meaning changes based upon the reference point or perspective of who is speaking. This ability to take different perspectives is difficult for most individuals with ASD.

The nonverbal aspects of language are typically affected in individuals with ASD. They have difficulty using their tone of voice, facial expressions and body language (gestures/ movement) to express meaning or feelings. They have difficulty knowing how close or far to stand when communicating, where to look or touch someone. Their vocal patterns are often characterized by a robot-like or monotone voice. Some individuals have a high-pitched or "sing-songy" quality to their voice.

At the opposite end of the spectrum there are those individuals whose speech and language difficulties affect only the higher-level aspects of communication. They may be able to speak in grammatically complete sentences, use appropriate vocabulary and syntax, but their ability to effectively use their language skills for social communication can be mildly to severely impaired. In addition, these individuals usually have difficulty not just in the use of their own language, but also in understanding the social language of others. They have difficulty recognizing and interpreting the subtle aspects of communication, such as tone of voice and nonverbal cues. Comprehension of humor and sarcasm are negatively affected, as these individuals typically don't appreciate their meaning or purpose.

Pragmatic (social) language problems can occur at the lowest as well as highest end of the continuum of behaviors. These types of problems might include but are not limited to poor eye contact, turn-taking skills, perseverating on a topic of self-interest with little or no regard for the listener, self-talk, lack of references for what is being said, and interrupting.

16   Are savant skills common in Autism?

No. Most Autistic individuals do not have savant skills. Savant refers to exceptional or extraordinary skills in particular areas that others do not typically have. According to some estimates, savant abilities occur in approximately 10% of the Autistic population compared to less than 1% in the rest of the population.

Most people think of the movie *Rain Man* when they think of Savants because the character played by Dustin Hoffman had savant skills. His skills focused around numbers: he could quickly count items at a glance, could count cards (remember when he and Tom Cruise went to Las Vegas?), recall names and numbers from the telephone book and recall schedules and dates. Often calendar skills are seen in Savants who can tell you what day any particular date falls on regardless of the year. Savant skills are often seen in these mathematical abilities but also in other abilities such as a general memory for facts, artistic and musical abilities.

17   What is Theory of Mind Deficit or Mindblindness?

Theory of Mind (ToM) was an idea proposed by Drs Simon Baron-Cohen, Alan Leslie and Uta Firth in the mid 1980s as a way to explain the difficulties experienced by individuals with ASD in appreciating other people's perspectives. The term "Mindblindness" was introduced by Dr Baron-Cohen in 1990. Essentially, the problem is in the person's ability to take the perspective of another person. Understanding that other individuals have different thoughts, feelings, likes, dislikes and points of view from the individual with ASD is often difficult for them. They frequently only see the world through their own eyes, referred to as an egocentric perspective, and they become frustrated and confused when others do not know what they know, see what they see, perceive what they perceive, or experience what they experience. Because of these difficulties in appreciating that other people think differently than they do, individuals with ASD have significant social deficits. This is also due to difficulty in predicting others' behaviors, reading others' intentions and motives, difficulty understanding and interpreting others' emotions, and not appreciating how their own behavior affects others.

Carol Gray developed a technique called Social Stories that has been used to help teach individuals with social deficits about what is expected of them in certain contexts and how others may perceive the same social situation. This technique is discussed in further detail in question 75 on social skills deficits.

I frequently use a tool called "barrier games" during speech and language therapy sessions to address ToM deficits. Barrier games are a therapeutic strategy that can address many goal areas simultaneously in treatment, including Theory of Mind. The basic premise of a barrier game is to provide a situation in which the individual with ASD can see how other people think and perceive things differently. This allows for an experiential learning rather than intellectual or cognitive learning. In other words, the individual actually experiences in a concrete way how someone thinks differently than he or she does and then learns how to change this limiting perspective. This is done, for example, by trying to replicate a block pattern from a verbal description alone, with no visual cues because of a barrier between the participants. The clinician and client each have the same blocks available and one describes to the other how he or she is building a tower. Without asking for clarification and by simply assuming one knows what the other person is thinking, the block towers are often built quite differently. Once the barrier is removed, the individual with ASD is provided with an immediate and concrete example of how what he/she was thinking was different from the clinician's thoughts. The clinician uses this opportunity to "debrief" the client and goes through the process of what was done and what could have been done differently. Teaching how to observe and ask relevant questions is a critical component to learning to understand others' perspectives. This type of barrier activity also provides a means to address a plethora of other language goals, targeting many issues associated with communication problems simultaneously (e.g., expressive language, grammar, linguistic concepts, language comprehension, memory, etc).

18 What are Executive Function Deficits?

Executive Function refers to those processes in the brain that are primarily responsible for problem solving and goal attainment. When people refer to executive functioning they are typically implicating the pre-frontal lobes (behind the forehead) of the brain. These are associated with the executive functioning skills such as organization and planning, set maintenance and change (i.e., starting and stopping tasks); flexibility (i.e., adapting to a context); and self-monitoring and inhibition (i.e., resisting an impulse). Executive Function Deficits are not unique to ASD. These difficulties are also seen in individuals with Attention Deficit Disorders, Obsessive–

Compulsive Disorder, Tourette's Syndrome and Childhood Schizophrenia.

Strategies such as role playing, teaching organization skills, teaching sequencing and planning skills and teaching cause and effect thinking to "stop, think, and then act" are typical interventions for individuals with Executive Function Deficits.

19 What are Central Coherence Deficits?

Central Coherence is the ability to "get the point." It is putting many pieces of information together to make sense of the whole picture in a particular context. Individuals with ASD often have difficulty with Central Coherence because of their idiosyncratic focus of attention (paying attention to irrelevant details); an imposition of their own perspective (only seeing things from their point of view); preference for familiar things; difficulties with making connections between concepts/ experiences and previous learnings; generalizing information not specifically taught to them; and difficulties making choices and organizing themselves.

Strategies for helping individuals with Central Coherence Deficits include: making the beginning and ending of tasks clear; avoiding ambiguity; teaching choice making and building opportunities for generalization; and making connections to previous learnings.

20 What are Nonverbal Learning Disabilities (NLD)?

Nonverbal Learning Disabilities (NLD), also called Nonverbal Learning Disorder, is a neurobehavioral disorder characterized by motor, social and visual-spatial organizational difficulties. NLD is also described by a pattern of associated assets or strengths. These include: early and precocious language skills; early development of reading skills (including Hyperlexia); excellent rote memory skills; strong auditory learning and retention of auditorily presented information.

NLD was first described in the 1960s as researchers began to notice children who had difficulty with social-emotional and math skills. It was not until the late 1980s that neuropsychologist Bryon Rourke published the first book on the subject. Rouke described five major areas of dysfunction in these children that were also seen in individuals who had damage to the right brain hemisphere. There are no entries in the DSM-IV or ICD-10 which identify NLD as a separate diagnostic entity, but researchers and clinicians have written about the similarities and differences between NLD, AS and Higher Functioning Autism. The ability to differentiate these diagnostic labels is currently being debated and further research is underway which may clarify matters.

From a practical viewpoint, many of the approaches and strategies used to treat any one of these disabilities will likely also be appropriate for the others. It is critical, however, that the individual be considered whenever interventions are developed because what works for one individual may or may not work for another. Despite many of the similarities seen in these populations, the ways in which they use their visual systems can be quite different. For example, many HFA and AS individuals utilize their visual system as a strength and support for learning, yet this is the same system that is dysfunctional for the NLD individual.

21 What is Hyperlexia?

Hyperlexia literally means extra or exaggerated words. It refers to a syndrome in childhood that has three primary characteristics: a precocious reading ability, significant difficulty in understanding verbal language, and abnormal social skills. These children typical learn visually, seek out consistent patterns or routines, have strong memory and imitation skills, are concrete and rigid thinkers, have highly focused interests and have difficulty with social interactions. These characteristics are also typically found in individuals who have ASD. As in many of the other diagnostic labels described in this book, the differences and similarities between conditions often overlap. Some professionals believe Hyperlexia is a distinct syndrome, while others consider it to be either one of the pervasive development disorders or the same as ASD. Some describe Hyperlexia as a symptom within ASD. It is not currently listed in the DSM-IV or ICD-10 as a diagnostic entity in its own right.

22 What is Pathological Demand Avoidance Syndrome (PDA)?

PDA was first identified as a pervasive developmental disorder related to, but significantly different from Autism and Asperger's Syndrome, by Professor Elizabeth Newson at the University of Nottingham, UK, in 1983. The diagnosis of PDA is not currently recognized in the DSM-IV or ICD-10 and is neither a common term nor established syndrome described in the peer-reviewed ASD literature. However, Professor Newson and her colleagues are conducting ongoing research at the Early Years Diagnostic Centre in Nottingham in an attempt to establish empirical support for their observations.

According to Professor Newson, the components which distinguish PDA from Autism and Asperger's Syndrome are as follows. PDA children are *less likely to*: have caused anxiety in their parents before 18 months of age; show stereotypical motor mannerisms; show or have shown echolalia or pronoun reversal; show pragmatic problems; show or have shown tiptoe walking or show compulsive adherence to routines. Additionally, PDA children are *more likely to*: resist demands obsessively; be socially manipulative by age five; show normal eye contact; show excessive lability of mood and impulsivity; show social mimicry; show role play and show other types of symbolic play. Fifty per cent of them are female (i.e., there is no significant gender difference in children with PDA).

The diagnostic criteria for PDA described by the Early Years Diagnostic Centre in Nottingham include:

1.   *Passive early history in first year.* Everything must be on his or her own terms as the child often resists normal demands (which, during the first year, are not often made, so differences are not as obvious at this age).

2.   *Continues to resist and avoid ordinary demands of life.* The child seems to feel excessive pressure from normal expectations and demands and, therefore, actively avoids direct demands placed upon him or her.

3.   *Surface sociability, but apparent lack of sense of social identity, pride or shame.* There is no sense of

boundaries, personal responsibility, negotiating or concern for fitting in with peers.

4. *Lability of mood, impulsive, led by need to control.* The child may quickly change moods as a result of needing to control a situation and can be impulsive in his or her behavior.

5. *Comfortable in role play and pretending.* The child is able to take on various roles that allow him or her to feel more in control, such as role playing a teacher or, during an assessment, wanting to be the examiner.

6. *Language delay, seems result of passivity.* The child's speech content may be odd or bizarre but he or she has less problem with pragmatics or eye contact.

7. *Obsessive behavior.* This is particularly noticeable with social obsessions like blaming or harassing people the child doesn't like, or overpowering those the child does like with affection.

8. *Neurological involvement.* There is not enough hard evidence for identifying specific neurological involvement, although some soft neurological signs such as clumsiness and crawling late have been observed in more than half the children studied.

According to Professor Newson, the important point in identifying PDA as a separate diagnostic entity from Autism and ASD is recognizing that these children require different intervention strategies (both educational and therapeutic). For example, PDA children require fewer rules and restrictions and more flexibility on the part of the adults working with them. Some of these strategies include utilizing indirect suggestions rather than direction, providing choices rather than structure, and reducing the "active passivity" seen in these children by encouraging them to take control in those instances where it is possible to give them control.

Only time will tell whether PDA will prove to be a separate diagnostic entity or part of a larger ASD picture as research continues to investigate these labels.

PART 2

Causes

23. What causes ASD?

24. Is ASD genetic?

25. Is there an ASD gene?

26. What are the chances of having more than one ASD child?

27. Can immunizations/vaccines cause ASD?

28. Can parenting style cause ASD?

29. Are there environmental causes of ASD?

30. Does a chemical imbalance in the brain cause ASD?

31. What medical conditions can cause ASD?

32. Can "Leaking" or "Leaky Gut" cause ASD?

33. What is the Opioid Excess Theory?

23   What causes ASD?

We don't know, but probably many different things. There are many studies in progress examining this question, but the only thing agreed upon is that it is likely to be a complex answer involving genetics, biology and neurology in combination with a number of environmental factors (before or after birth). One thing we know for certain is that parenting style (good, bad or indifferent) does not cause ASD!

As research continues to examine the etiology of ASD, it is becoming more apparent that there may be a variety of causes because there may be a variety of different kinds of ASD, some of which are not yet clearly identified. Some ASDs may have a stronger genetic basis than others. For example, Rett Syndrome, which typically occurs in girls, is of genetic origin. Studies of twins and family histories are ongoing and have shown a higher incidence of Autism and Autistic symptoms in family members. Research has not identified a single gene that is responsible for any ASD, and so it is presumed that there is a combination of genes and other factors (pre-existing conditions), which are likely to be involved. Chromosome 7 continues to be prominently implicated in the research but the extent to which it will be documented as a cause of Autism has yet to be discovered. See questions 24, 25 and 26 for further discussion about ASD and genetics.

There are several medical conditions such as Fragile X, William's Syndrome, Landau-Kleffner Syndrome, Tuberous Sclerosis and others, which can manifest as ASD. Any condition that affects the central neurological system's development is a potential cause of ASD. This includes pre-natal (before birth), peri-natal (during the birth process), and post-natal (after birth) events. For example, viral infections (e.g., Encephalitis, Congenital Rubella); metabolic problems (e.g., Phenylkentonuria); exposure to toxic substances to the fetus or developing child (e.g., chemicals such as lead, mercury, alcohol, drugs); oxygen deprivation; birth trauma; subsequent head trauma; seizure disorders and numerous other biological factors may be implicated in ASD.

Much attention has recently been given to the consideration that vaccinations, the MMR vaccine in particular, may be a cause of Autism. The research results are conflicting based upon the methodology of the studies, although the response from parents who comment upon the change in their child after the MMR is less wavering. More studies are underway and some policy changes are beginning to take place regarding doctors being able to administer single doses rather than all three simultaneously, depending upon which country you live in. Japan eliminated the use of the combined dosage of the MMR vaccine in 1993. For more information about the MMR vaccination, see question 27.

Another line of research addressing the causes of ASD relates to gastrointestinal (GI) difficulties due to the many ASD individuals with GI problems (see question 29). This has led to some controversial studies on the use of Secretin as a treatment to address the GI problems and subsequently reduce the ASD symptoms (see question 44). Definitive results are yet to be available on this new line of research.

There is much we are learning, but much yet to be learned in the quest to seek out the causes of ASD. For some websites which may be helpful to you in keeping up on current research into the causes of ASD, see question 81.

24 Is ASD genetic?

Most often, the research studies at this time relate to a genetic *susceptibility*, rather than a genetic *cause* to Autism. This may eventually change as research continues in this area. The genetic studies done to date often indicate that the children with Autism in a particular study may have a particular genetic marker that is higher in these children than those without Autism. However, the genetic markers are not consistently found to be the same across all studies of individuals with Autism.

Most experts agree there is a strong genetic component to ASD. But what we don't know is how much is genetic and how much is influenced by other factors. Nor do we know yet which types of ASD have a stronger genetic basis than the others.

Twin studies have been especially useful in recognizing the importance of the genetic components of Autism. This type of research gives a basis for the strong genetic component of Autism, since identical twins share 100% of their genes, while fraternal twins and non-twin siblings share significantly less. Depending upon which studies are reported, there is a 60–95% chance that if one identical twin has the diagnosis of Autism, so will the other. But with fraternal twins the chances of both being diagnosed with Autism are about the same as non-twin siblings, about a 5–8% chance.

Beyond the twin studies indicating a genetic basis for Autism, 10–15% of individuals with Autism are estimated to have another genetic disorder, such as Fragile X or Tuberous Sclerosis. Genetic testing can be valuable to determine whether another genetic disorder is present.

25   Is there an ASD gene?

No. There is no single gene that causes Autism or Autism Spectrum Disorders, but family studies and especially studies of twins indicate there is a significant genetic component to ASD. As research continues in this area, it is not likely that a single gene will be found, but there will probably be several genes and factors which together cause Autism. Current studies suggest there may be a complex interaction among 3 to 15 or more different genes associated with ASD. There are several ongoing research studies examining which specific genes and chromosomes may play a part in the development of Autism Spectrum Disorders, and several regions of interest to researchers studying genes. One of the chromosomes that are often implicated in studies of Autism is chromosome 7, but it is not specifically known how or what genes may be affected. In addition, we do not yet know how the relevant genes may be inherited.

The amount of current research in this area is great and beyond the scope of this book to describe. Only a few of the current studies are reported here to give you some general information, but science at this time does not provide us with information to identify or treat Autism based upon genetics. There is promise in the studies that are being undertaken that some day may assist better early identification, prevention and treatment.

Chromosomes 2 & 7

Researchers from the US and Europe screened the DNA of 150 pairs of siblings with Autism. They identified strong evidence for implicating chromosomes 2 and 7 for containing genes that are involved in Autism. They also found a correlation with chromosomes 16 and 17.

The RELN gene

Researchers studying the reelin protein (RELN gene) have found approximately 20% of Autistic subjects carry a long version of the gene that could have come from either parent. This gene is reported to possibly increase the risk of a child's developing Autism by age three. The assumption is that there is a reduced level of reelin in the brain. Post-mortem studies of Autistic individuals confirm this hypothesis in those subjects studied. Reelin has previously been studied in connection with Bi-polar Disorder and Schizophrenia.

ADA2 & DBH

A risk factor for the development of Autism has also been associated with a gene variant known as ADA2 which results in low activity of the ADA gene (adenosine deaminase). Another study found that in mothers who had two or more Autistic children, DBH (dopamine beta-hydroxylase) occurred more frequently than in control subjects and the DBH enzyme activity was reduced in the mothers compared to the controls.

HLA and chromosome 6

Researchers at Utah State University have found genes on chromosome 6 (known as human leukocyte antigens or HLA), which they say are linked to the occurrence of Autism. They also report the tendency toward Autism as inherited from the father. This is in contrast to several studies that have indicated that the number of symptoms of Autism is higher when this gene is inherited from the mother.

MeCP2

Rett Syndrome has been attributed to the mutation of a gene (MeCP2) although not all individuals with Rett's have a mutation of this gene. Researchers at Duke University also recently reported that some individuals with Autism have MeCP2 mutations.

WNT & DVL and chromosome 7

There are several studies of mice exhibiting reduced social interaction similar to that seen in Autism, which are associated with the gene families WNT and DVL. In addition, mice with abnormalities in brain development similar to individuals with Autism supposedly caused by a teratogen such as Thalidomide or alcohol before birth are associated with a HOXA1 gene mutation. These genes are located in the region of chromosome 7, which has previously been associated with Autism in many other studies.

26   What are the chances of having more than one ASD child?

With our current incomplete state of knowledge concerning the causes of ASD, there is no clear-cut answer to this question. Depending upon the research reviewed, there is anywhere from a 3 to 8% chance of having a second child with Autism once you have had one child with Autism. This is about 50 to 100 times the normal risk of having more than one ASD child. If you have identical twins, one of whom is diagnosed with Autism, the chance that the other will be diagnosed with Autism, even if they manifest different levels of severity or behaviors, is anywhere from 60 to 95%. As research continues, there may one day be a test that helps parents better understand their own genetic makeup in order to know what the specific chances are for them to have another child affected with ASD.

Family studies of children with Rett Syndrome showed a rare recurrence of having a second child with Rett Syndrome (less than 0.4%).

Family studies have been useful in describing how similar patterns of behaviors and cognitive characteristics are seen in family members of Autistic individuals to varying degrees. This is referred to in the literature as Broad Autism Phenotype. One sibling may have Autism while another may be affected with language problems, social impairments or stereotyped behaviors, but to a lesser degree and therefore not qualify for one of the ASD labels.

27   Can immunizations/vaccines cause ASD?

This issue came to the forefront in the late 1990s when Andrew Wakefield, a gastroenterologist then working in London, England found that 12 Autistic children developed an inflammation in their intestines and regressed in their abilities after receiving the Measles-Mumps-Rubella (MMR) vaccination. After his findings were published in the British medical journal, *The Lancet*, many parents reported similar findings and the controversy and further research began.

The research to date has not supported a relationship between the MMR vaccine and Autism, but many concerns about the research methodology and the conclusions drawn have resulted in continuing the research. Some of the factors suggesting to some that the MMR vaccine plays a role in ASD are the type of Autism it appears to contribute to (Regressive Autism), the timing of vaccines (e.g., the young age at which they are given), the multi-dose rather than a single dose administration, and (in the United States) the uncertain effects of adding Thimerosal to the vaccines. Thimerosal is a preservative, containing almost 50% mercury, that is used to prevent fungal and bacterial contamination in some multi-dose vaccines. Mercury has been a known toxin for some time.

Although the research to date does not support a direct link between the MMR vaccine and autism, the observations and common experiences reported by physicians and families keep the research alive.

The Collaborative Programs of Excellence in Autism (CPEA) were started in 1997 to address the neurobiology and genetics of Autism. One of their many avenues of study relates to the relationship between the MMR vaccine and a possible cause of Autism. For more information about the CPEA's work and other research studies by the National Institute of Child Health and Human Development (NICHD), which is part of the National Institutes of Health (NIH), visit www.nichd. nih.gov/autism. Other websites for further information about vaccines and Autism are listed at question 81.

28   Can parenting style cause ASD?

Definitely *not*. Unfortunately, there was a time in the not too distant past when Autism was poorly understood and the false belief was that Autism was caused by so-called "refrigerator moms." This term referred to a cold, uninvolved, parenting style that suggested the lack of emotional connection between mother and child was at the root of Autism. There was never any scientific evidence for this viewpoint and with increased knowledge and subsequent research it could be proven that there was a physical basis to the diagnosis. We now know, without any doubt, that parenting style is not the cause of Autism Spectrum Disorder. And yet some countries still believe in this theory despite all the evidence to the contrary. In fact, the 2001 edition of the Italian Rizzoli-Larousse encyclopedia still referred to the "refrigerator mother" theory of Autism, which was withdrawn following a campaign by outraged Italian parents.

Many children with ASD, especially those severely impaired, show limited or no response to their parents and so it is easy to see how parents can fall into the cycle of not responding positively to their children or limiting their involvement. That is a terrible mistake. These children need the extra support and involvement of parents who care and will help to create the best possible environment to help them develop to the best of their abilities.

29 Are there environmental causes of ASD?

The evidence suggests there are. It is generally agreed upon that both internal and external factors are relevant in the expression of Autism Spectrum Disorders. This is sometimes referred to as a gene–environment interaction. The research continues, but currently most literature describes an underlying susceptibility to ASD that, in some cases, can be triggered by environmental conditions. Environmental factors can include different kinds of events that can impact a fetus (before birth) or an infant or child (during or after birth). The primary environmental areas that are being researched include: infections, antibiotics, vaccinations, allergies and toxins.

The infections most often associated with Autism can occur in either the pregnant mother or in the child. There is anecdotal evidence of several different infections in pregnant women who have subsequently given birth to a child with ASD, including: Rubella, Herpes, HIV, Cytomegalovirus and Epstein-Barr. Children's infections have also been associated with Autism, including Encephalitis (a swelling of the brain tissue which can be a complication of measles and mumps); otitis media (ear infections); yeast and streptococcus bacteria (that can cause strep throat, for example). These infections are obviously not unique to Autism, however.

It has also been suggested that the use of broad-spectrum antibiotic treatments for various infections in childhood may lead to the destruction of beneficial flora (e.g., bacteria) found in the intestinal tract. The relevance of this observation is that chronic intestinal infection can produce neurological symptoms consistent with Autism in some individuals. The relationship between intestinal problems and Autism is explored in more detailed in question 32, which addresses a phenomenon referred to as "Leaky Gut."

There is a large amount of research being undertaken to determine the role that vaccinations play in the development of Autistic symptoms. This is especially true for the Measles-Mumps-Rubella (MMR) vaccine. The concerns primarily surround the metal toxicity associated with mercury found in Thirmerosal, a preservative in some vaccines. The conclusion of some scientific research has been that vaccines do not cause Autism. Other researchers, however, continue to study this issue due to the well documented scientific evidence of mercury poisoning and their beliefs that the conclusions drawn are incorrect due to flawed methodology in the studies.

Allergies may be associated to Autism through a reverse process. By treating the allergy to specific foods (e.g., milk products, gluten) and then seeing a reduction in Autistic symptoms, some have associated allergies to ASD.

Pollutants and toxins in the environment and their effect on children's hearing, behavior, sensory, motor and mental development are also being studied for their possible link to ASD. Previous scientific research in the area of lead poisoning, for example, has shown a relationship between environmental toxins and subsequent learning, behavior and attention deficits. The direct link with ASD is under investigation.

30 Does a chemical imbalance in the brain cause ASD?

At this time, the evidence is inconclusive. There is ongoing research into the various neurotransmitters that seem to be involved in Autism Spectrum Disorders. Neurotransmitters are the chemical messengers in the brain that carry information from one cell to another. There are dozens of different types of neurotransmitters, such as Dopamine, Acetylcholine and Serotonin. Some research suggests that approximately 25–50% (depending which research is considered) of Autistic individuals have an elevated amount of Serotonin in their brains. Higher Serotonin levels are not unique to ASD. They have been found in other conditions as well and so the relationship between elevated Serotonin and Autism is not yet clear. However, it has led many researchers to study the effects of the use of medications called Selective Serotonin Reuptake Inhibitors (SSRIs) as a form of intervention. The SSRIs include: Fluoxetine (Prozac), Fluvoxamine (Luvox), Paroxetine (Paxil), Sertraline (Zoloft) and Citalopram (Celexa).

31 What medical conditions can cause ASD?

A number of different medical conditions can cause or create patterns consistent with ASD. A list of some of these disorders is provided below.

- Angelman Syndrome

- Brain injury

- Cornelia de Lange Syndrome – abbreviated as CdLS, also called Brachmann-de Lange Syndrome (BDLS)

- Congenital Rubella

- Down's Syndrome

- Duchenne Muscular Dystrophy

- Fragile X (FRAXA)

- Landau-Kleffner Syndrome/Acquired Epileptic Aphasia

- Nonverbal Learning Disabilities

- Prader-Willi Syndrome

- Tuberous Sclerosis (TS)

- Williams Syndrome

32 Can "Leaking" or "Leaky Gut" cause ASD?

It is not yet clear. "Leaking" or "Leaky Gut" refers to the phenomenon that occurs when there is inflammation or damage to the gastrointestinal tract, which in turn may allow peptides to get into the bloodstream and ultimately into the brain. Whether "Leaky Gut" is a cause of Autism for some individuals is still highly debated and under investigation. See question 43 for further information on "Leaky Gut".

33 What is the Opioid Excess Theory?

This theory suggests that foods are not correctly digested in the body and as a result peptides work their way into the bloodstream and eventually into the brain causing an increase in opioid activity in the brain. This effects the neurotransmission (or communication) within the brain causing a disruption of normal brain activity and producing the symptoms of Autism. The presence of opioid peptides also affects the immune system and hormonal regulation. Proponents of this theory subscribe to the "Leaky Gut" theory described in the previous question.

PART 3

Medical Issues

34. Can ASD be identified before birth?

35. Can ASD be identified at birth?

36. Are specific parts of the brain affected in ASD?

37. Is the immune system affected in ASD?

38. Is the gastrointestinal system affected in ASD?

39. What role do environmental toxins and viruses have in ASD?

40. What role do allergies play in children with ASD?

41. What is the "DAN" protocol?

42. What is "PANDAS"?

43. What are "Leaky Gut" and "Celiac Disease"?

44. What is Secretin?

45. Do all children with ASD have seizures?

46. How do I know if my child is having seizures?

47. What medications are used with ASD individuals?

48. What is Purine Autism?

49. What is the Urine Peptide Test?

34   Can ASD be identified before birth?

No. Genetic research suggests there are susceptible spots on some chromosomes (e.g., 2, 6, 7, 15, 16, 17), but at this time they do not either predict or confirm a diagnosis of ASD. There may be a time in the future when genetic screening will help predict who will be susceptible to ASD, but currently there are no such tests or screening devices available.

35   Can ASD be identified at birth?

No, not yet. But in May 2000, at the American Academy of Neurology meeting, a preliminary study was introduced that holds promise for early identification. The researchers identified four brain proteins that are crucial in the development of the nervous system, which may identify Autism and Mental Retardation. They are: V.I.P., NT-4, CGRP and BDNF.

The pilot study, conducted by lead researcher Dr Karin Nelson, did lab tests on blood samples taken from newborns born between 1983 and 1985 in the San Francisco Bay area who were later diagnosed with Autism, Mental Retardation or Cerebral Palsy. There were 60 children in each group, including an unaffected, or control, group. Ninety-five percent of the children later identified as Autistic or mentally retarded had strikingly high levels of these four specific proteins. Few of the children with Cerebral Palsy and none of the controls had these high levels. This study was considered highly significant because of its potential for early identification of children with

Autism and Mental Retardation.[1] Further studies must be conducted to replicate these findings before a screening tool can be devised for newborns to detect these or any other biological markers at birth.

36 Are specific parts of the brain affected in ASD?

There is no conclusive evidence that one particular part of the brain is abnormal in *all* Autistic individuals. It has only been since the 1980s that researchers have been able to identify specific brain abnormalities evident in some Autistic individuals compared to the non-Autistic population. With the advent of newer brain scanning technologies and more research into the area of the neuro-anatomy of Autism, we are just beginning to understand some of the relationship between the brain and Autism.

The first studies using MRI neuro-imaging technology identified a structural defect in an area of the brain called the vermis, located in the cerebellum (the part of the brain located at the back of the head). Subsequent studies have implicated other brain structures such as the pons, amygdala and hippocampus.

Autopsy studies have identified many different areas involved in the brains of Autistic individuals not seen in a control group. Some of those studies have found: a reduction in Purkinje cells; granule cell loss in the cerebellum; and various

1   For more information on the study conducted by Karin Nelson, contact the March of Dimes–California Birth Defects Monitoring Program on (00 1) 888-898-2229 (in the United States) or at www.cbdmp.org.

size and density issues of cells in the hippocampus, amygdala, anterior cingulated cortex, among other areas.

Some studies have begun to associate specific brain abnormalities with specific functional deficits. For example, abnormalities of the amygdala are suspected to contribute to social and emotional dysfunction, and dentate abnormalities could affect memory functions. There is still much research to be done to replicate such studies before conclusively associating a brain structure with a functional deficit in particular individuals.

Recently, there have been studies using functional Magnetic Resonance Imaging (fMRI) whereby an individual engages in a task while simultaneously having their brain scanned in order to see which parts of the brain "light up" or show activity during the task. Some studies have found that brain activity in some individuals with Asperger's Syndrome is different than the "normal" population when engaged in a task where they have to figure out what someone else is thinking or feeling. Additionally, a study done in London identified a relationship between the prefrontal lobes and obsessional behavior and social function in individuals with Asperger's Syndrome. Other studies have demonstrated low functional activity of a temporal lobe structure called the fusiform gyrus in Autistic subjects when viewing faces. Autistic subjects show that they are unable to quickly, frequently and accurately shift attention back and forth between disparate stimuli (such as sights and sounds).

Such sophisticated research continues, but there are no firm conclusions that can be made yet regarding a specific brain structure or structures, either damaged or not developed, that consistently cause ASD in all individuals.

37   Is the immune system affected in ASD?

Studies of some Autistic children have shown a compromised immune system. The white blood cells can be sluggish and weak. An autoimmune process in which the body attacks itself has been suggested in those Autistic individuals whose antibodies to brain proteins are more prominent than in the "normal" population.

One of the current lines of research is studying the effects of the Measles virus antibodies and how they may trigger an autoimmune response that interferes with the development of myelin in the brain. Myelin is necessary for the electrical connections between cells in the brain.

Usually, a physician will order blood to test for autoimmune disorders. There are several different types of tests a physician might choose from based upon the individual being tested. Some of these are listed below.

- *Amino acid profile*: Looks for markers that the immune system is compromised.

- *Anti-neuronal antibody (ANA) screen*: A test to look for antibodies to brain tissue in the bloodstream.

- *Blood count*: Looks for whether the white blood cells are depleted.

- *Chemistry panel (Chem)*: A number of different tests can be performed in a chemistry panel. Typically, checking levels of glucose (sugar), creatinine and electrolytes are done in a basic chemistry panel.

- *Colonoscopy*: Looks for lower GI tract problems. Performed by a gastroenterologist.

- *Immune panel test*: Looks for specific immune-dysfunction markers.

- *Immunoglobulin G (IgG) tests*: Looks for specific viruses or conditions affecting the immune system.

- *Sedimentation rate (Sed rate)*: Looks for how quickly the red blood cells separate from the serum in a test tube.

The role of the immune system in ASD has been highlighted by the Autism Research Institute in their Defeat Autism Now (DAN) conferences. A clinical protocol has been established from these meetings, called the DAN protocol, that is available from www.autismresearchinstitute.com for any doctor to follow. More information about the DAN protocol can be found in the answer to question 41.

38 Is the gastrointestinal system affected in ASD?

Some individuals with ASD have gastrointestinal problems that are often most noticeable by parents as problems with constipation or diarrhea. The actual difficulties in the gastrointestinal tract are often associated with what has come to be called "Leaky Gut." This occurs when there is inflammation or damage to the gastrointestinal tract (creating tiny holes) which then allows peptides to get into the bloodstream and ultimately into the brain. Peptides are protein particles that come from various foods. Some individuals with ASD have difficulty handling the proteins from milk products, wheat or other grain products. For this reason, diets that are gluten and/or casein free (GF/CF) have been tried with some success to reduce or eliminate gastrointestinal problems. Further research in this area is ongoing and needed to state conclusively which individuals may benefit from which diets and what types of changes can be expected as a result.

Using enzymes to help with digestion and to counter the effects of foods (peptides) getting into the bloodstream has recently been getting some attention in Autism literature. Enzymes are a special type of protein that the body uses in all chemical reactions. Using this approach, enzymes are chosen on the basis of which types of foods need to be broken down to result in better digestion and the healing of the gastrointestinal tract. The four types of enzymes used for breaking down the various types of food are: amylase to break down carbohydrates; cellulase to break down fiber; disaccharidases to break down sugars and protease to break down proteins.

39   What role do environmental toxins and viruses have in ASD?

It is unknown at this time, but environmental toxins and viruses are suspect in the cause and maintenance of ASD symptoms. Chemicals that are toxic to the developing brain are called developmental neurotoxicants. We have known for decades that various toxic chemicals can negatively impact a child's neurological development. Learning disabilities, attention deficits and behavioral disorders have been associated in some cases with children having been exposed to these environmental pollutants (e.g., lead poisoning).

The relationship between environmental chemicals and Autism began surfacing in the literature in the 1980s and more recently, in the late 1990s, there has been an increase in the awareness of metal toxicity in individuals with ASD. Some of the common metals being associated with symptoms consistent with ASD include: aluminum (Al), antimony (Sb), arsenic (As), lead (Pb), cadmium (Cd), mercury (Hg), nickel (Ni) and tin (Sn).

A hair analysis is typically the most non-invasive means of determining metal toxicity. There has been some controversy about the quality of analysis and the findings between various laboratories so caution is warranted in pursuing this analysis and as with all consumer information it is important that you get references and do your homework before proceeding.

If metal toxicity is suspected, Chelation Therapy may be recommended. This is considered an alternative treatment and not supported by the traditional medical community in treating individuals with ASD. However, Chelation Therapy is a medically approved treatment for lead poisoning. Chelation is a means for detoxification and involves an individual ingesting an oral chelating agent (different substances are available for this purpose) which supposedly binds to the toxic metals and is then eliminated from the body.

40 What role do allergies play in children with ASD?

Allergies are not unique to individuals with ASD, and they do not seem to cause Autism although some individuals suggest allergies as a culprit in the ASD profile. Allergies are the result of the immune system perceiving something as toxic to the system and then attempting to counter it. Allergies can take several different forms and be caused by any agent. Whether the reaction is to pollen, yeast, peanuts or anything else, it can affect your skin (rashes); your eyes (dry or teary, puffy, itchy, dark circles underneath); your nose (congested, runny, itchy) or cause swelling in any part of the body. Some people report that behavioral changes may also be symptoms of allergies.

Allergies are treated by first identifying what the foreign substance is that causes the body to overreact and then finding the appropriate treatment. Your physician or a specialist such as an allergist can order different types of tests to determine whether allergies are present and what you might be allergic to.

Food allergies, such as getting a rash when one eats strawberries, may be different from the individual who appears unable to tolerate grains or dairy products (discussed in questions 38 and 43). The difference is about determining whether there is an immune system response or a metabolic disorder. Elimination diets are often used to determine whether an individual is sensitive to a particular food. Whether considered an allergy or a metabolic disorder, the result is usually the same: remove the offending food substance from the person's diet or the allergen from the person's environment, if possible.

Research in this area is ongoing and needed to state conclusively which individuals may benefit from which diets and what types of changes can be expected as a result.

Some individuals suggest that "food allergies" in individuals with ASD are really more likely food intolerances and a result of poor digestion. This idea is consistent with those proponents of the "Leaky Gut" theory of ASD described in question 32. Use of enzymes (special proteins involved in chemical reactions in the body) is often suggested as a line of treatment to reduce the assumed digestive problem. The scientific literature is limited.

41 What is the "DAN" protocol?

The DAN protocol is an alternative (non-pharmaceutical) medical approach to the diagnosis and treatment of Autism.

In 1995 Dr Bernard Rimland of the Autism Research Institute and his colleagues, pediatrician Sidney Baker, MD, and chemist Jon Pangborn, PhD, organized a conference called Defeat Autism Now (DAN). The gathering of physicians and researchers from the US and Europe achieved a consensus on a natural approach for diagnosing and treating children with Autism, which was published in a manual, *Clinical Assessment Options for Children with Autism and Related Disorders: A Biomedical Approach*. The clinical manual has been revised numerous times and provides among other things, a list of biomedical laboratory tests, procedures for submitting samples, preferred labs for analysis of test results, and flow charts for deciding on diagnostic and therapeutic strategies. The DAN protocol is used by physicians who do not support psychotropic drugs as the best or only means of treating Autistic individuals. The most current DAN protocol can be obtained from the Autism Research Institute (www.autism researchinstitute.com). A list of DAN physicians is also available at this website.

42 What is "PANDAS"?

PANDAS is an acronym for Pediatric Autoimmune Neuropsychiatric Disorder Associated with Streptococcus (PANDAS). The PANDAS project, conducted by the National Institute of Mental Health's Dr Susan Swedo, identified a bacteria-triggered autoimmune response as the basis for some cases of childhood neuropsychiatric illness. One of the findings of this study, which led to further study of the role of the immune system in ASD, was that a blood marker (B lymphocyte antigen D8/17) was associated with PANDAS. The hope is that it might yield a diagnostic blood test for ASD in the future.

43   What are "Leaky Gut" and "Celiac Disease"?

"Leaking Gut" refers to the process that occurs when there is inflammation or damage to the gastrointestinal tract (creating tiny holes), which then allows peptides to get into the bloodstream and ultimately into the brain. Peptides are the protein particles that come from various foods. Some individuals with ASD have difficulty handling the proteins from milk products, wheat or other grain products. For this reason, diets that are gluten and/or casein free (GF/CF) have been tried with some success. Research in this area is ongoing and needed to state conclusively which individuals may benefit from which diets and what types of changes can be expected as a result.

Use of enzymes (special proteins involved in chemical reactions in the body) is also being tried to address digestion problems by helping the body break down certain foods with particular enzymes. These include: amylase for carbohydrates, cellulase for fiber, disaccharidases for sugars and protease for proteins. The scientific literature is limited in this regard and no evidence is yet available for how best to utilize enzymes in an Autism treatment regime.

The intestinal permeability test can determine whether a person has a "leaky gut" by having them drink a solution and then analyzing their urine. Additionally, urine can be analyzed in a lab to check for the presence of abnormal peptides associated with gluten and casein (see question 49). Some individuals believe that simply putting a child on a GF/CF diet and observing changes is a valid way to determine "Leaky Gut" without having to go through any other tests. Others believe medically determining whether "Leaky Gut" is an accurate diagnosis is an important first step before restricting a child's diet.

Proponents of the use of enzyme supplementation suggest that individuals may not need a restricted diet if the enzyme can assist in the breakdown of certain foods so that the peptides do not get into the bloodstream.

There is another medical condition, an autoimmune disease called Celiac Sprue, sometimes called Celiac Disease, which is an inflammation of the small intestine's lining. The inflammation can result from various sources, such as overgrowth of Candida yeast, use of antibiotics or autoimmune conditions. Individuals with Celiac Disease have difficulty digesting many everyday foods and have chronic diarrhea or unusual stools. This is not a unique condition to those with ASD.

44 What is Secretin?

Secretin is a hormone necessary for normal digestion. It stimulates the pancreas to produce digestive enzymes and bicarbonate. Single injections of Secretin have been used for many years as a diagnostic tool regarding digestive system function. It came to the forefront of the Autism literature in the late 1990s when Gary and Victoria Beck told their personal story about their Autistic son Parker on television shows in the United States.

The Beck story revolves around their son Parker's medical condition of unresolved gastrointestinal problems. They consulted with a gastrointestinal specialist who performed a Secretin challenge test during a medical procedure called an endoscopy and found Parker had a chronic inflammation of the bowel. Parker's immediate response to the Secretin was to produce five times the volume of digestive enzymes expected. However, within the weeks and months that followed administration of the Secretin, Parker had another response that eventually jump-started the Autistic community. He began to speak and quickly went from a two-word vocabulary to speaking hundreds of words. His parents also reported a significant improvement in Parker's eye contact and social interaction. The two years of diarrhea that Parker had struggled with ended and he became toilet trained.

Parker's story prompted parents to begin the search for information and doctors who might administer Secretin. What developed, though, was inconsistent use of the hormone in various forms including types of administrations and variable dosages without any controlled studies of its efficacy. After Parker's story hit the media and parents were knocking on doctors' doors to obtain Secretin, controlled research began to investigate whether Secretin really was a valuable form of treatment for Autism and whether it was safe to use.

To date, despite occasional anecdotal reports of success, the studies have not yet made a strong case for the scientific validity of Secretin. Studies that have been conducted in using Secretin with Autistic individuals have varied too much in their methodology to yield clear results. Different forms of Secretin have been used in the different studies; the type of administration (IV, oral) has varied; and the dosages (amount and number of times Secretin was administered) have not been consistent between the studies. Parents continue to report anecdotally the benefits of Secretin and more research is needed. The Autism Research Institute in San Diego, California has been tracking parent information and maintains records of families willing to complete a Secretin Outcome Survey.

There are several different types of Secretin. Ferring Secretin, which came from pigs, was once the sole source of

Secretin, but its production was stopped in 1999. This left meager amounts of Secretin available and most of the leftovers were used in clinical trials. The Ferring Secretin was considered 60% pure. Another type is porcine Secretin imported from Japan to the United States. The first synthetic Secretin, called SecreFlo, was approved by the United States Food and Drug Administration (FDA) in April 2002 for pancreatic diagnosis. In contrast to Ferring Secretin, the new synthetic Secretin is 99.6% pure. The company that will market SecreFlo, RepliGen Corporation, is the one conducting clinical trails of Secretin and Autism. This leads some to believe there is a conflict of interest and so, predictably, the studies will be questioned. However, the Food and Drug Administration (FDA) of the United States is also evaluating Secretin at five major medical centers.

45 Do all children with ASD have seizures?

About a third of individuals with ASD have some type of seizure disorder. When ASD children reach adolescence, there is an increase in the number of individuals who experience seizures. These are often managed with anti-convulsant medications and can stop by the time these individuals reach adulthood.

Some children with neurological conditions, such as Tuberous Sclerosis, which manifests itself in behaviors similar to those with ASD, are at higher risk for seizures. Additionally, individuals with Landau-Kleffner Syndrome, sometimes called Acquired Epileptic Aphasia, have seizures as one of the identifying characteristics of their diagnosis.

46   How do I know if my child is having seizures?

Most people think of a seizure as the dramatic type called tonic/clonic seizures (previously called Grand Mal seizures) in which a person's entire body begins to convulse or shake, and he or she may lose consciousness. If your child has had this kind of seizure you will know it. There is nothing subtle about it. There are several different types or kinds of seizures, however, some of which are very difficult to detect or notice. Individuals with ASD, like the general population, can have any type of seizure disorder.

There are several types of generalized seizures that can affect the whole brain, including: absent seizures, myoclonic seizures, atonic seizures and the tonic/clonic seizures described above. Absent, or Petit Mal seizures, are the least likely to be observed unless you know the characteristics to observe and document the episodes for consultation with a neurologist. These seizures are very brief in length, usually occurring for less than ten seconds, and may only be observed by a staring episode or eye blinking/twitching. Since this behavior can sometimes be observed in someone without the presence of seizures, it is important to write down when these behaviors are observed and how long they last so that you can take this information to your physician who may then refer you to a neurologist for EEG testing. Myoclonic seizures are characterized by jerky movements of muscles. Atonic seizures result in a person being unable to stand or sit upright due to a loss of muscle tone.

There are also partial seizures which affect only part of the brain. These include simple partial and complex partial seizures. Simple partial seizures will affect one part or one side of the body and may include twitching uncontrollably, a feeling of confusion or disorientation, and possibly the individual may hallucinate sights, sounds or smells, but remains conscious. Complex partial seizures are like simple partial seizures but also include a loss of consciousness.

Seizures are diagnosed through clinical symptoms and EEG (electroencephalogram) results. EEGs produce a graph/print-out of the electrical output of the brain measured by putting electrodes on the exterior of the head. There are different types of EEGs that a physician may order, including awake EEGs, asleep EEGs, 24-hour EEGs, etc, depending upon the reported symptoms and concerns. An EEG only reports the electrical activity in the brain *at the time* the individual is hooked up to the machine. So, it is possible an individual may have a negative EEG (indicating no seizure activity), but may actually be having seizures at other times. That is why it is so important that you monitor and document behaviors and mannerisms as well as when they occur in order to help provide your physician with the information he or she needs to determine what type of EEG to order. In addition, based upon your observations and the individual's symptoms, a physician may often order a repeat EEG to try to "catch" a seizure when it happens.

Seizures are typically treated with anti-convulsant medications. Which medication to use, of the many available, and the dosage to take is a decision made by your physician. In some cases, corticosteroid therapy or special diets like the ketogenic diet are also considered for individuals with seizures, especially those with Landau-Kleffner Syndrome.

47   What medications are used with ASD individuals?

There are no specific medications designed to either treat or cure ASD. The medications commonly used are for symptom management only. Therefore some individuals with ASD are not taking any medications, while others take several medications. The studies on the use of drugs for children and the ASD population are increasing, but most of the drugs prescribed have not yet been approved for use with children or specifically for the ASD population. The decision whether to take medications to alleviate various symptoms is a decision for individuals and their physicians.

The medications prescribed for individuals with ASD are used for specific symptom management, such as attention and behavior. Therefore, the same drugs prescribed to treat the attentional issues of children with ADD or ADHD are used with ASD children. Similarly, drugs used to treat the maladaptive behaviors, such as self-injurious behaviors and temper tantrums, have been used with depressed, anxious or psychotic patients.

Many of the current medications that are used to treat anxiety and depression, called Selective Serotonin Reuptake Inhibitors (SSRIs), are used with the ASD population for management of behavior. These drugs include Fluoxetine (Prozac) Fluvoxamine (Luvox), Sertraline (Zoloft), Paroxetine (Paxil) and Citalopram (Celexa). SSRIs may help reduce agitation and aggression and increase an overall tolerance for changes, according to some studies.

Another group of drugs, referred to as neuroleptics or anti-psychotic drugs, has also been used in the ASD population to reduce agitation, aggression and repetitive behaviors. Drugs such as Chlorpromazine (Thorazine), Theoridazine (Mellaril), and Haloperidol (Haldol) are strong and can produce severe and possibly permanent neurological side effects. Therefore their use is typically for a temporary reduction in the problem behaviors rather than long-term use.

A newer group of drugs is the atypical neuroleptics, which have fewer side effects than the neuroleptics. This group includes such medications as Clozapine (Clozaril), Olanzapine (Zyprexa), Risperidone (Risperdal), Quetiapine (Seroquel) and Ziprasidone (Zeldox).

There are other medications that have been used with ASD populations that are too numerous to mention here. A list of medications in Appendix F includes some of the drugs described here, and additional information about them. This is not a comprehensive list of every drug available. And, with new drugs still in development, more options will likely be available in the future.

48   What is Purine Autism?

Purines are chemical compounds found in the waste product of uric acid. They are most commonly known for causing gout. Purines have various roles in the body: converting genes to proteins, converting energy for cell use; serving as messenger chemicals; as antioxidants protecting against cancer-causing agents; and they help to get rid of excess nitrogen. Given these multiple purposes in the body, there are a number of different kinds of purine metabolism diseases. Their effect on the body can range from asymptomatic to fatal. Metabolic disease is tested for in blood work ordered by your physician.

Some children diagnosed with Autism have been found to have an overproduction of purine compounds in their urine.

There has been no specific enzyme defect identified thus far to account for this. Research is underway to study this condition.

49 What is the Urine Peptide Test?

The Urine Peptide Test is a method of testing for gluten and casein intolerance by looking for abnormal peptides in the urine. Many parents simply bypass the test for various reasons (ranging from time, cost and false negative findings) and instead choose to eliminate gluten and casein products from a child's diet. If there is improvement after the elimination diet is implemented, then a test is not necessary. Some parents, however, find it hard to stick to the diet. Knowing conclusively with a lab test that your child has intolerance may make it easier to stick to the diet. Many people, however, suggest that it doesn't matter what the lab tests show since the diet may have positive effects even without any evidence of abnormal peptides in the urine.

PART 4

Treatments and Intervention Programs and Approaches

50. What types of treatment approaches exist for ASD?

51. Are all treatment approaches equally beneficial?

52. How do I decide which intervention(s) are most appropriate for my child?

53. What are Applied Behavioral Analysis (ABA) and Discrete Trial Training (DTT)?

54. What is Pivotal Response Training (PRT)?

55. What is Floor Time and the Developmental, Individual Difference, Relationship-based approach (DIR)?

56. What is the SCERTS Model?

57. What is TEACCH?

58. What is Speech-Language Therapy?

59. What is Augmentative Communication (AC) and PECS?

60. What is Auditory Integration Training (AIT)?

61. What is Occupational Therapy (OT)?

62. What is Sensory Integration Therapy (SI)?

63. What is Physical Therapy?

64. What is Art Therapy?

65. What is Animal Assisted Therapy?

66. What is Music Therapy?

67. What is Vision Therapy?

68. What diets are used to treat ASD individuals?

69. What vitamins and nutritional supplements are used with ASD individuals?

70. What is Immunotherapy?

71. What medications are used to treat ASD?

72. How is Melatonin used in treating ASD?

73. Are there specific interventions for toilet training?

74. Are there specific interventions for temper tantrums?

75. Are there specific interventions for social skills deficits?

76. Are there specific interventions for sleep disturbances?

77. Are there specific interventions for self-injurious behaviors?

78. Are there specific interventions for auditory processing problems?

50 What types of treatment approaches exist for ASD?

There are different types of treatments that can be effective in helping to reduce the symptoms associated with ASD. The purpose of answering this question is to provide the reader with the types of treatment approaches available, while the answer to the next question will address whether all treatment interventions are equally beneficial. Not all the interventions currently in use have been empirically supported with scientific data, but some people have reported success with them nonetheless. With ongoing study, eventually we may learn which types of interventions will be best for which types of ASD.

The following list of treatment approaches and methods can be divided into various categories depending upon how you view intervention. Whether you consider treatment according to place of intervention, the person intervening, or the area focused upon will determine how you might categorize these treatments. Although research has usually addressed a single treatment approach, anecdotal reports suggest that most families engage in more than one type of intervention. It is important to differentiate a specific intervention technique or strategy from a general treatment approach. A strategy is a specific method within a type of approach. For example, speech and language therapy is a treatment approach, while using social stories is a strategy to use in speech and language therapy.

The following is a list of some of the treatment approaches currently being used with ASD individuals. The list below includes various treatment methods, traditional and nontraditional, scientifically validated and not.

Acupuncture

Acupuncture is a part of traditional Chinese medicine and, as such, has not been well studied or easily accepted into cultures that are based upon westernized medicine. In the world of Autism, even less is known about the effects of acupuncture.

Animal Assisted Therapies (horses and dolphins)

As the name states, these therapies utilize animals to interact with the individual. It is generally considered a non-traditional, complementary form of intervention for individuals with ASD and various other special needs populations. No empirical data are available at present regarding the use of Animal Assisted Therapies with individuals with ASD. Refer to question 65 for further information about this approach.

Art Therapy

Art Therapy is another less traditional, complementary form of intervention for individuals with ASD. Art Therapy is not a vehicle for turning individuals into artists, but instead strives to help individuals increase their communication skills, develop a better sense of self, build social relationships and facilitate sensory integration. No empirical research supports Art Therapy for individuals with ASD. Refer to question 64 for further information about this approach.

Auditory Integration Training (AIT)

There are several different methods of AIT (e.g., Berard, Tomatis, SAMONAS). These techniques involve having an individual listen to specially created CDs to enhance or develop the auditory system. There is no empirical research supporting this approach. Refer to question 60 for further information about AIT.

Augmentative Communication (AC)

This approach is designed to facilitate communication in individuals who are not able to use speech as their primary means of communicating. It includes both low and high technology approaches such as sign language, Picture Exchange Communication System (PECS) and computers. Refer to question 59 for further information about this approach.

Discrete Trial Training (DTT)

Also known as "the Lovaas method", this is a behaviorally based intervention initially developed as a research instrument by Ivar Lovaas at UCLA in the 1960s. DTT uses structured activities, specified behaviors and rewards in a 1:1 setting. Empirical research supports this and other related behavioral approaches. Refer to question 53 for further information about this approach.

Education

Educational intervention can range from segregated schools, designed specifically for individuals with ASD or other special needs, to involvement in mainstream classrooms.

Floor Time

This approach is based upon play therapy approaches and the Developmental, Individual Difference, Relationship Model (DIR) developed by Dr Stanley Greenspan and Serena Wieder. The underlying philosophy of this approach is to help the child make an emotional connection to his world. There is no specific empirical research supporting this approach with ASD individuals. Refer to question 55 for further information about this approach.

Medications

There is no medication specific to treating Autism. But medications are used to treat various symptoms associated with Autism such as behaviors (aggression, obsessive/compulsive), hyperactivity, anxiety and attention. The empirical research for medication varies with the medication and the specific symptoms for which they are prescribed as well as for the age of the individual. Refer to question 71 and Appendix F for further information about medications.

Music Therapy

Music Therapy is another less traditional and complementary intervention for ASD individuals. It is not designed to teach how to play a particular musical instrument. Rather, it is a vehicle or modality for emotionally connecting with the individual through music and then teaching other skills necessary for daily living, such as cognitive, motoric and linguistic abilities. There is limited research on the use of Music Therapy with ASD. Refer to question 66 for further information about this approach.

Occupational Therapy and/or Sensory Integration Therapy

Occupational Therapy is a form of treatment that focuses on the skills necessary for daily living. This usually includes addressing three different areas: self-care, sensory motor and fine motor skills. Sensory Integration Therapy is a specialized means of intervention that focuses on the brain's ability to interpret the information from the senses. Research supports Occupational Therapy services for some motor impairments, but fewer empirically supported data are available for Sensory Integration Techniques. Refer to questions 61 and 62 for further information about these approaches.

Physical Therapy

Physical Therapy is a form of treatment that addresses the rehabilitation of gross motor skills. Physical Therapy is an empirically supported treatment for specific motor deficits. Refer to question 63 for further information about this approach.

Pivotal Response Training (PRT)

PRT is an approach developed by Drs Laura Schreibman and Robert Koegel based upon behavioral principles and the natural language paradigm. The emphasis is on teaching an individual the pivotal skills associated with communication (e.g., motivation) to facilitate their development in a variety of areas (play skills, social skills, language development). PRT is based upon empirically supported research. Refer to question 54 for further information about this approach.

Speech-Language Therapy

This discipline utilizes various approaches to facilitate all aspects of communication including: the physiological aspects such as respiration and oral-motor skills, speech (articulation/pronunciation), language comprehension, language expression (vocabulary, grammar, syntax), pragmatic language (social language), voice, fluency and Augmentative Communication. There is a strong base of empirically supported data for Speech-Language Therapy in the ASD population. Refer to question 58 for further information about this approach.

Structured teaching – the TEACCH program

TEACCH is an acronym for Treatment and Education of Autistic and Related Communication Handicapped Children. It is a highly structured program developed in the early 1970s by Eric Shopler at the University of North Carolina. It is an educationally based approach, which includes specific classroom methods, involvement of community agencies and support services for families. It is based upon empirically supported research gathered over a span of more than 20 years. Refer to question 57 for further information about this approach.

Vitamins, diet and supplements

The scientific literature is currently in its infancy regarding the efficacy of using vitamins, diet and nutritional supplements as a treatment method for ASD. Anecdotal reports and scientific data have been accumulating for only the past decade and include a plethora of information about what does or doesn't work, but the results are mixed. It isn't known which vitamin, supplement or combination of the two might be effective for specific individuals. The Autism Research Institute in San Diego has compiled data from thousands of parents, providing numerous anecdotal reports and scientific studies that support a non-medication approach to resolving symptoms and improving quality of life for ASD individuals. There is much more to learn about the effect of vitamins, supplements and diets and whom they will be most effective with for changing or eliminating ASD symptoms. Refer to questions 68 and 69 for further information about this approach.

The HANDLE Institute approach

HANDLE is an acronym for Holistic Approach to Neuro-development and Learning Efficiency. The HANDLE Institute approach was originated 30 years ago by educator Judith Bluestone in order to provide a holistic, non-drug alternative for diagnosing and treating many neuro- developmental disorders. The HANDLE approach focuses primarily on various types of sensory stimulation (exercises and activities) for individuals with ASD. There are many personal and professional testimonials about the HANDLE approach but no scientific data supporting its specific use for individuals with ASD has yet been reported. See www.handle.org for further details.

The Linwood Method

The Linwood Method was developed in the 1950s by Jeanne Simons for a residential program in the United States for Autistic individuals. It was described in detail in her book *The Hidden Child: The Linwood Method for Reaching the Autistic Child* (Woodbine House, 1986). The approach used in this method is to develop an individualized program that addresses the underlying motivations behind behaviors rather than treating symptoms alone.

The Options Institute Method ("The Son Rise Program")

The work of Barry and Samahria Kaufman with their own son, Raun, is the foundation for The Options Institute. They designed their own intensive stimulation program based upon an attitude of unconditional love and acceptance. Barry Kaufman has written about their experience in his books *Son-Rise* (Warner Books, 1976) and *Son-Rise: The Miracle Continues* (H.J. Kramer, 1995). Kaufman's latest book *No Regrets: Last Chance for a Father and Son* is expected to be published this year (2003). The Kaufmans report that after three years of this constant stimulation and effort in joining Raun in his own world, he no longer shows any signs of his Autism. First developed in Massachusetts, there are now Options Institutes in Holland and the UK. The Institutes offer training for families wishing to replicate the Kaufman's work. Controversy surrounds this approach, however, because it is very expensive and requires a level of intensity that few people can provide. There are no scientific data supporting this approach.

51 Are all treatment approaches equally beneficial?

No, not all treatment approaches are equally beneficial for treating ASD. However, some approaches have been helpful for some individuals despite the fact that they have not been well supported by scientific research (at least not yet). That doesn't mean they don't work. It just means there isn't clear evidence that they do. Which approaches will work best for which individuals? The answer is not yet known.

There is no "one size fits all" treatment approach that will be appropriate for all individuals with ASD. Each individual manifests his or her symptoms differently. Thus, the ultimate decision about which approach or approaches to use must be highly individualized. Furthermore, since ASD can have many causes and many different types of symptoms, it usually requires many different forms of treatment.

Behavioral approaches have been given the most attention in the research and have been used the longest so more is known about the value of those approaches. They have been shown to be highly effective in controlling or eliminating many symptoms as well as developing new skills in individuals with ASD. Many peer-reviewed research studies are available on the efficacy of behavioral approaches. These approaches are described in more detail in question 53.

In more recent research, empirically supported studies have demonstrated that naturalistic approaches that consider the child's choice, follow the child's lead and use natural reinforcers in the context of therapy are just as effective, if not more so, in developing communication, social skills and behavioral symptom management or elimination than the traditional behavioral approaches. Naturalistic approaches can be applied in different interventions such as Speech-Language Therapy or Pivotal Response Training (PRT). See questions 58 and 54 for further information on these treatment approaches.

The TEACCH program is an empirically supported approach in the educational environment. This program is described in more detail in question 57.

Many of the interventions being considered and used today do not have rigorous and detailed accounts of their efficacy for individuals with ASD. Some approaches have had only a few studies while others have had more published research, but the results remain inconclusive. It is one thing to study a hypothesis in a research context but a very different thing to account for all the possible variables that will allow something to work with individuals diagnosed with ASD. The variability in these individuals can be great, and research studies have difficulty accounting for all the possible human contingencies that present themselves to tell us what will work and with whom. However, it is promising to note that the amount of research into the area of ASD is steadily increasing, offering us valuable information from which we can make informed decisions.

For many of the treatment approaches described for ASD the scientific community is divided. Studies are criticized for various reasons, which can range from valid scientific concerns such as the methodology of the study, to errors arising from personal stakes in maintaining face or financial gain. A single study can be interpreted differently depending upon who is drawing the conclusions. Therefore, it is most important for you to learn as much as you can before proceeding with any one approach.

52 How do I decide which intervention(s) are most appropriate for my child?

Most often, multiple interventions are necessary for a successful program. Even the definition of what a "successful program" is varies. For some, success will be the total elimination of ASD symptoms while for others success may be defined as an increase in responsiveness, an ability to communicate or a reduction in self-injurious or aggressive behaviors. Parents must be critical thinkers and good consumers when they choose a program for their children. Parents need to be patient about their child's progress but at the same time they need to regularly evaluate the success of interventions so they may be flexible in recognizing when there may need to be a change of tactics. This is a hard set of demands to place on parents when they may be at an especially emotional time in their lives as they deal with a child (or children) with ASD.

There are many programs out there with little or no evidence to support their often exaggerated claims. Although some of these people and programs may genuinely believe in their approach, others are simply taking advantage of emotionally vulnerable parents by promising what they cannot deliver. If any of the following unsupportable claims are made to you, it would be wise to avoid the program or approach.

- "This program is guaranteed to cure your child's Autism."

- "This program has worked for every child who has been in the program."

- "This program is the *only* way to help your child."

- "I can't support any program other than this one."

- "You don't need to work with any other professionals if you participate in this program."

In order to determine the most effective approach for a given child, it is important that a parent or professional consider that child's individual needs. That may seem an obvious statement but, too often, parents may hear of an approach that has worked for one child and then hope or even assume that it will work for their child as well. Many times parents have come to my office asking about a program or approach they have heard about from another parent, believing it will work for their child because of only one or two similar symptoms the two children happen to share.

It is often necessary to provide treatment on multiple levels (e.g., education, speech therapy, behavioral intervention, Sensory Integration Therapy) and no single approach or program is sufficient. In evaluating which program fits your needs or that of your child's, here are some questions you may want to ask to help guide your decision:

1. What specific areas of difficulty am I, or is my child, experiencing and will this program/approach address those areas? How will it do this?

2. What specific strengths do I, or does my child, have and will they be addressed or utilized in this program/approach? How will it do this?

3.   Is there any scientific evidence for this program/approach? Where can I read more about it?

4.   Who is involved in the direct service to me/my child? Are these licensed professionals? Will there be aids or support staff working with me/my child?

5.   Will the program/approach address my or my child's needs outside of the setting in which the program is administered? How will generalization occur?

6.   To what extent are parents, spouses or other family members involved in the program?

7.   How much time and money will be invested in this program?

8.   What criteria are used to measure my or my child's progress?

Additionally, it is important that you ask for the credentials and experience of anyone who will work with you or your child. You can find out whether the individuals have advanced degrees in their educational backgrounds such as a Master's degree (MA, MS) or a doctorate (PhD), whether they are licensed by a governing board that adheres to ethical guidelines of behavior and holds licensees responsible for their actions, and the number of years of experience they have or what their expertise is in a particular area.

53 What are Applied Behavioral Analysis (ABA) and Discrete Trial Training (DTT)?

ABA and DTT are terms associated with the work of Dr O. Ivar Lovaas (Professor Emeritus, Psychology, UCLA) who developed an intensive intervention program for Autistic children in the 1960s using principles based on Applied Behavioral Analysis (ABA). The general goal of this approach is to train a child to give a new behavioral response to a specific stimulus based upon positive and negative consequences, also referred to as either reinforcement or, simply, reward and punishment. The only "punishments" used in the program today are social rather than physical, such as saying "no" or giving "time outs."

The first step in a Lovaas program is to observe the child and develop a plan to change behaviors. To do this, you observe the behaviors that require change or modification, attempting to determine what factors lead to the undesirable behavior, and what consequences of the behavior serve to reinforce or keep the behavior going. By simply observing, you find out what level the child is currently functioning at before treatment, called a baseline. Next, you develop goals in order to determine which particular behaviors will be addressed in treatment. Next, you break down the new behaviors into smaller steps and teach the specific skills necessary to develop them. The individual steps are taught in discrete units that have a specific beginning and end. These are repeated in multiple trials during any single session in order to condition the new behavior. For this reason, the term Discrete Trial Training became synonymous with ABA. However, ABA refers to a research methodology based on behavioral principles and is not a treatment in and of itself.

The basic components of a DTT program include the following:

- Intensive training is given in the home from 30–40 hours a week.

- Direct services are provided in a one-on-one context.

- Behaviors are broken down into discrete tasks.

- Tasks are repeated until achieved before moving on to more difficult tasks.

- A child is rewarded for each instance when a desired behavior is demonstrated.

Some of the advantages of this systematic approach are a clear set of expectations, breaking tasks into small attainable parts, and teaching attention to task. Some of the disadvantages include the considerable time demands; the limited generalization of skills beyond what is conditioned; the potential for learned helplessness and prompt dependence; a focus on learning to respond rather than initiating; task redundancy; and the reliance on artificial reinforcements not likely to be found elsewhere in daily life.

There is much more to such programs than has been so briefly described here. Scientific evidence has lent substantial support to the use of behavioral approaches such as DTT in working with individuals with ASD.

54   What is Pivotal Response Training (PRT)?

Pivotal Response Training, or PRT, was developed by Drs Robert Koegel and Laura Schreibman. It is considered a behavioral treatment based upon applied behavior analysis principles. This approach also uses discrete trials to teach behaviors, but its emphasis is more child centered and the rewards are based upon a natural contingency to the task. For example, in getting a child to say the word "car," a discrete trial trainer may provide a child with a candy, hug or sticker for saying the word. But a person doing PRT would provide the child with a toy car that was labeled as "car." PRT works to increase motivation by including components such as allowing the child to make choices in the treatment such as what activity or task to engage in, turn-taking, positively reinforcing attempts and not just success, and interspersing maintenance tasks or those skills already acquired.

Dr Schreibman directs the Autism Research Laboratory at the University of California San Diego (UCSD). Along with others, she has been studying the PRT approach in targeting language skills, play skills and social behaviors in children with Autism. There are many ongoing studies being conducted at the lab pertaining to parent training, peer involvement, siblings, and examining which children would most likely benefit from PRT approaches.

55 What is Floor Time and the Developmental, Individual Difference, Relationship-based approach (DIR)?

Floor Time is the intervention strategy associated with the Developmental, Individual Difference, Relationship-based approach (DIR) developed by Dr Stanley Greenspan and Serena Wieder. Floor Time gets its name because one of the identifying characteristics of DIR is that the adult gets on the floor and plays with the child.

Floor Time is more, though, than just being on the floor and playing. It has underlying principles that serve to motivate and guide the interaction with the child. These revolve around facilitating communication and problem solving and include:

- following the child's lead

- joining the child at his or her developmental level

- building on the child's interest and then motivating the child to build on what the adult has said or done (referred to as opening and closing circles of communication)

- finding individual ways of reaching the child emotionally.

Floor Time was developed as a means to achieve the principles of the DIR approach that strives to focus on the whole child. The philosophy of the DIR approach is based on the need to develop a child's emotional connection to people and the world in order to develop in other important areas. The underlying difficulties experienced by children are assumed to relate to biologically based sensory processing issues. These are best addressed by three basic principles of the DIR approach which are reflected in the name of the model.

1.   *Developmental:* This principle deals with the child's emotional, social and cognitive developmental levels. The DIR approach identifies six stages of development that a child needs to master in relating to others.

2.   *Individual Differences:* This principle addresses the uniqueness of each child and tailoring an individual approach that takes a child's specific pattern of behaviors into account.

3.   *Relationship based:* This principle is the basis of the DIR approach in recognizing and emphasizing the child's emotionally based interactions.

An advantage of Floor Time approaches is that they include multiple components of development in functional wholes and do not only address individual parts or symptoms. Furthermore, it incorporates a child's interests and emotions and is therefore tailored to a specific child and not his or her diagnostic label.

56 What is the SCERTS Model?

SCERTS is an acronym for Social Communication, Emotional Regulation and Transactional Support. It is an educational/ treatment approach for enhancing communication and socio-emotional abilities in individuals with Autism Spectrum Disorders. The SCERTS model was developed by a team of individuals including speech language pathologists: Barry Prizant, PhD, Amy Wetherby, PhD, Emily Rubin, MS, Patrick Rydell, PhD, and occupational therapist, Amy Laurent, OTR/L. It was designed to provide an integrated approach to working with ASD individuals across various settings. This approach is derived from the collaborators' 25 years of research, clinical and educational experience and incorporates empirical research and sound clinical/educational practice from children with and without disabilities.

57 What is TEACCH?

The TEACCH method was developed in the early 1970s by Eric Shopler at the University of North Carolina. TEACCH is an acronym for Treatment and Education of Autistic and Related Communication Handicapped Children. It is a highly structured program that includes specific classroom methods, involvement of community agencies and support services for families. Many schools around the world have used the structured teaching methods of the TEACCH program. It includes a systemic way of organizing the environment, scheduling and teaching methods. It is based upon sound research and program efficacy is continually being evaluated.

One of the most common methods taken from the TEACCH program is the use of visual schedules. These are essentially a visual way to organize the child's world for him or her by listing with pictures, symbols or words what the sequential steps are for the child to follow throughout the day or for a given period of time. This organization and sequencing of behaviors helps provide a structure for a child who might otherwise be stressed or highly agitated by not knowing what to expect or to do next.

Some of the advantages of TEACCH are that it is an individualized, multi-dimensional treatment, it doesn't necessarily subscribe to only one methodology, and it encourages and helps develop greater independence. Some of the possible disadvantages are that it is potentially too structured with its reliance on routines, it is typically offered in a segregated educational setting, and it encourages an intra-dependence rather than an appropriate inter-dependence that might facilitate more social interaction.

58   What is Speech-Language Therapy?

Speech-Language Therapy is a form of treatment used either to eliminate or to help compensate for delays and deficits in communication. Since speech and language problems are primary symptoms in the diagnosis of ASD, this discipline is often involved in intervention programs.

Individuals with ASD can require Speech-Language Therapy for many different types of problems. Difficulties with communication can range from being nonverbal and unable to use speech at all to communicate, to the other end of the continuum in which an individual is highly verbal yet unable to grasp certain concepts or engage appropriately in social skills. The ability to communicate effectively requires an array of skills that are addressed in Speech-Language Therapy. Some of these include:

- speech (articulation or pronunciation of sounds)
- oral-motor skills (ability to use the muscles of the mouth to produce sounds as well as to eat)
- voice (rate, volume, rhythm)
- fluency (stuttering)
- expressive language (using grammatically and syntactically complete sentences to express thoughts, ideas and feelings)

- receptive language (understanding language or language comprehension)

- pragmatic (social) language

- body language (gestures, facial expressions)

- auditory processing skills (the ability of the brain to make sense of what the ear hears)

- attention and behavior.

Some of the common problems experienced by individuals with ASD who require Speech-Language Therapy include:

- lack of speech

- regression of speech

- unintelligible speech due to muscle coordination or muscle strength problems (including dyspraxia, apraxia, and dysarthria)

- monotone voice

- echolalia

- pronoun confusion

- incomplete sentences

- poor or limited vocabulary

- grammar and syntax errors

- limited or poor language comprehension

- difficulties following directions

- auditory memory problems

- poor ability to sequence thoughts and ideas in a meaningful way and maintain thought organization

- social skills deficits ranging from the lack of ability to make or maintain eye contact to lack of turn-taking skills and inability to use language for engagement with others and appreciating various perspectives.

These areas are often addressed in Speech-Language Therapy as pragmatic language problems.

The list of potential issues to be addressed in Speech-Language Therapy is quite extensive and beyond the scope of this book. There is substantial research evidence that Speech-Language Therapy is effective in helping reduce communication problems associated with ASD. Good Speech-Language Therapy should be highly individualized and based upon the specific needs of the person, their ability level, their motivation and interests.

59   What is Augmentative Communication (AC) and PECS?

Most people have heard of or seen renowned physicist Stephen Hawking. He has advanced Amylotrophic Lateral Sclerosis (ALS) and has minimal use of his body. This neurological disorder prevents him from using his voice to speak. Instead, he communicates by using a personal computer system referred to as Augmentative Communication (AC), sometimes called "alternative communication" or "assistive technology." It is a way for individuals to communicate who are either nonverbal or whose speech is significantly impaired and limited in its use.

Prior to the advent of computers, Augmentative Communication was primarily accomplished through sign language and picture symbols and drawings. These low technology options continue to be excellent choices for many individuals who are not candidates for the higher technology options available in various computer devices. Sign language may be taught by a speech-language therapist, audiologist or teacher of the deaf. One of the drawbacks to using sign language with individuals with ASD is that their fine motor coordination and control is often affected and so making precise signs can be a skill too difficult for them to master. Parents are frequently concerned that if they teach their children sign language or use pictures to help them to communicate then they won't speak. Research has indicated just the opposite effect, however. By reducing the frustration of not communicating and reducing the pressure put on the oral system to produce speech, this can actually enhance or facilitate the opportunity for speech to develop (if it is going to).

PECS stands for Picture Exchange Communication System and is an approach developed by Lori Frost and Andrew Bondy. PECS involves using pictures to communicate. By beginning with simple, single words and then building to phrases and sentences and eventually more complex communication, the individual can effectively communicate without voice. The emphasis is on helping an individual develop the skills for *initiating* communication with other people. Visual symbols for a PECS program or other visual system can be purchased, but individuals can also make their own picture communication books with actual photos or simple drawings of relevance to a particular individual. PECS and other picture symbols are effective in the use of facilitating communication (initiating requests, questions and comments as well as responding to questions and comments from others) as well as for organizing a daily schedule. By putting pictures in a particular order, it can help an individual with ASD understand what events will take place during the day and in what order. This visual understanding of daily events can prevent many of the tantrums and frustrations experienced by the individual with ASD and are described in more detail in question 57 about the TEACCH approach.

The advent of computer technology has significantly advanced Augmentative Communication. Various devices are now available, in hand held as well as larger desktop computers, which can facilitate a nonverbal or speech impaired individual's ability to communicate. From simple to complex, these devices can be developed for the individual needs of a particular person based upon their physical and cognitive abilities. Individuals with motor impairments may need special devices or adaptations to be able to utilize a particular form of AC, such as touch screens rather than keyboards, or pointing devices rather than using their fingers. Some devices are programmable, others are not. Assistive technology specialists, speech pathologists and occupational therapists can be invaluable in evaluating which type of Augmentative Communication system is right for a particular individual.

One of the most controversial techniques for assisting nonverbal individuals was introduced in the 1980s in Australia (and in the 1990s in the United States) to help individuals with Cerebral Palsy. It is called Facilitated Communication (FC). This approach uses another individual, called the "facilitator", to provide physical support to the individual with ASD in order to allow him or her to point to the symbolic representation (pictures, numbers, keys on a keyboard, etc) to communicate. The use of the facilitator is what made this approach controversial. Research demonstrated that the facilitators, albeit unintentionally, were communicating their own thoughts and wishes, rather than that of the individual with ASD. There is no scientific validity to this approach. However, proponents of this approach who have found it to be beneficial to their children continue to support its use and thereby encourage others to consider it a useful tool in facilitating communication.

60 What is Auditory Integration Training (AIT)?

Hearing sensitivity (which can be either an over- or under-responsiveness to certain sounds) has been reported in the ASD literature for many years. The need to address this common symptom resulted in the development of Auditory Integration Training (AIT) in France by otolaryngologist, Dr Guy Berard. Since Dr Berard's initial development of AIT, there have been spin-offs and various modifications made so that many individuals now use the term AIT to mean any generic program that addresses the auditory system through listening to music. Therefore, I will briefly provide an overview of the underlying techniques of AIT, and then I will describe the variables associated with the three most common forms of AIT: Berard, Tomatis and SAMONAS.

In general, AIT involves listening to processed music through headphones for a designated period of time. This is done by a piece of equipment that attenuates the low and high frequencies randomly called "modulation." The music choice is based upon the range of sound frequencies, and is individualized according to the results of an audiogram (a hearing test that shows the levels at which an individual responds to certain frequencies). When the audiogram is initially given, any frequencies at which a person is hypersensitive show up on the graph as an "auditory peak." The goal of AIT is to reduce these peaks so that all frequencies are perceived equally well and the hearing system can better respond to the sounds in the environment.

We do not currently know who is considered a good candidate for AIT. There are some research studies that support its efficacy, but for whom and why it works are still not known. Reports of behavioral problems for some individuals have been noted including agitation, increased activity level and mood swings that were not observed prior to AIT. Positive changes have been reported as well, including an increased attention span, responsiveness in general to others, an increased ability to tolerate sounds in the environment and greater production of speech. Some reports indicate, however, that the positive effects are not sustained over time. There has been no research to date to indicate there is a benefit in repeating AIT once it has been tried. These are often referred to as "booster sessions." It is important to note that AIT alone does not purport to address all of the aspects or characteristics of ASD and results are considered most beneficial when a multidisciplinary team of professionals is involved with the individual receiving AIT.

The Berard method

The original Berard method uses one of two devices to filter and modulate music. These are called the AudioKinetron and the Earducator. The AudioKinetron is no longer generally available, but it is still used by some practitioners who use the traditional Berard method of AIT. The typical schedule for traditional Berard AIT is two half-hour sessions per day for 10–20 days.

The music used in the Berard method includes a wide variety of styles such as reggae, pop, folk, rock, new age and jazz. The idea, according to Berard, is to have a wide range of frequencies and a rapid beat. An "approved" list of music was developed by Bill Clark and agreed upon by Dr Berard.

Other devices have been developed and are used in what have been called "Berard-derived AIT approaches." They include: Digital Auditory Aerobics (DAA), the Electronic Auditory Stimulation effect program (EASe program), and the Kirby Auditory Modulation System (KAMS). These programs/devices vary in the type of music/sounds chosen and how it is modulated.

The Tomatis method

Another style of AIT was developed by Alfred Tomatis, a French otolaryngologist and psychologist. This approach, sometimes referred to as "Audio-Psycho-Phonology," considers the psychological component of listening along with the neurophysiological level by using the client's own voice and the mother's voice in some aspects of the program. The music is processed using the Electronic Ear and consists mostly of symphonies, Mozart violin concertos and Gregorian chants. In addition to listening through headphones (which send the signal through air conduction), the sounds are also presented through vibration (which sends the signal through bone conduction). With the Tomatis method, the program length varies with listening times ranging from 30 minutes to two hours a day. Overall the number of hours in a full program can range from 20 to 100.

Two additional Tomatis-based programs are called "Listening Fitness" (LiFT) and the "Listening Program." The LiFT program *is not* designed for children with ASD. The Listening Program includes baroque and classical music and emphasizes the speech range frequencies.

The SAMONAS method

SAMONAS is an acronym that stands for "Spectral Activated Music of Optimal Natural Structure." It was developed by Ingo

Steinbach in Germany and is based on the work of Dr Tomatis. The program varies from 8 to 16 weeks and the individual listens to both classical music and nature sounds.

Many different commercial products have been derived from the theories behind AIT. Consumers should carefully consider all information about product efficacy and discuss with a professional who does not promote the product what the cost/benefit ratio might be for a particular individual before considering its use.

61   What is Occupational Therapy (OT)?

Occupational Therapy is a form of treatment that focuses on the skills necessary for daily living. This usually includes addressing three different areas: self-care, sensory motor and fine motor skills. Self-care skills can include basic skills such as eating, brushing one's teeth and dressing oneself. The fine motor skills addressed in OT range from basic skills necessary for self-care (such as buttoning and tying shoes) to more complex skills, such as writing. Sensory motor skills address the vestibular system (associated with balance), the tactile system (touch) and the proprioceptive system (involved in knowing one's body position in space). For adolescents and adults, Occupational Therapy can also help work on independence and vocational skills. There is considerable scientific research that supports Occupational Therapy techniques. Individuals who provide this treatment are called occupational therapists. They have an advanced academic degree, and either a state license or credential, depending upon where they live.

For many individuals with ASD, a specialized form of Occupational Therapy, called Sensory Integration, is often necessary. See the next question, which further explains this form of treatment.

For more information about Occupational Therapy around the world, please visit the World Federation of Occupational Therapists website at www.wfot.org. It lists over 50 member countries, and allows you to click on any of these countries' websites for further information about Occupational Therapy in that country.

62 What is Sensory Integration Therapy (SI)?

Sensory Integration (SI) Therapy is based upon the idea that the body receives information through various senses and people with motor and sensory impairments (such as those seen in many individuals with ASD) have difficulty processing that information accurately. Disturbances in touch, movement, and balance are often addressed with SI. These are referred to as tactile, proprioceptive and vestibular problems respectively.

SI addresses issues such as tactile sensitivity in individuals who do not like to be touched, or who do not like the light touch of someone brushing up against them or the feel of certain textures, including those of certain clothing on their body. Other individuals appear not to respond to touch or pain, and SI helps them learn to recognize these sensations. Helping individuals tolerate various textures, whether in their hands, their mouths or on the body, is a goal of SI Therapy. Techniques such as brushing, deep pressure massage and exposure to various textures while increasing one's tolerance for them are some of the therapeutic methods used to address tactile sensitivity.

Proprioceptive difficulties are based upon the lack of information being sent to the brain from the muscles, joints and nerves. Common SI techniques for proprioceptive problems include joint-compression, swinging and jumping. Vestibular problems are associated with balance issues and are typically addressed through exercises of balance and crossing the midline (using the right hand/arm on the left side of the body and vice versa).

Using sensory integrative exercises can be helpful in desensitizing or increasing sensitivity to nerves in the mouth by trying various food textures and doing oral exercises. Some speech therapists also address areas associated with oral sensitivity.

SI Therapy is designed to address processing issues, such as how quickly a sensation reaches the brain, and how it is perceived or interpreted, how the person organizes or responds to the sensory information, and how it is integrated with past and present experiences. SI Therapy is based upon the theories first developed by an American occupational therapist named Jean Ayres. In order to provide SI Therapy, one must receive specialized training and obtain certification from Sensory Integration International.

"Sensory Diet" is a term used to describe daily exercises that are integrated into a person's schedule in order to have regular intervals of sensory stimulation that would not otherwise happen for this person. These can be a combination of simple or more complex exercises that can be done either independently or with the help of others.

Even within the field, individuals argue about how to specifically define SI. Because of this, research has been inconclusive about its effectiveness. Individual clinicians who use SI and parents have certainly supported it, but the scientific results vary depending upon how SI is defined. Additionally, according to SI principles, the procedures for SI include the need to adapt methods used according to the needs of the individual client. That makes scientific study very difficult because replication of a study is often impossible when individuality and response style of a particular person must be considered. Consequently, the current research does not yet support the efficacy of SI, but bear in mind that the lack of standardized research does not suggest it is not useful in individual cases.

63 What is Physical Therapy?

Physical Therapy specializes in developing strength, coordination and movement in the large muscle groups of the body. Physical therapists work on improving gross motor skills through structured and repetitive physical activities including exercise.

Physical Therapy is usually prescribed by a physician and is often delivered in medical centers and facilities. Depending upon the country you live in and how service responsibilities are divided, there are some individuals with ASD who work on their large muscle group and gross motor skills within the school districts through adaptive physical education programs. Funding issues usually determine how services are offered to individuals.

For more information about Physical Therapy around the world, visit the World Confederation for Physical Therapy website at www.wcpt.org.

64 What is Art Therapy?

Art Therapy, like Music Therapy, is a less traditional, complementary form of intervention. Some studies have suggested that it can be a useful means of breaking through the barriers of Autism by connecting with an individual emotionally and allowing for some personal expression even if nonverbally. Art Therapy is not meant to be a "cure," but rather is another vehicle for trying to reach ASD individuals and expand their means of communication, social interaction, self-confidence and sensory integration. Art is itself a form of communication, symbolic in nature, which can be a means of expanding other forms of communication in some individuals.

Typically, art therapists begin their training as mental health clinicians who then specialize in utilizing the medium of art to engage clients and help expand their skills. As with Music Therapy, the goal is not to develop the artistic skills of the individual or turn them into an artist as much as to use those skills to address other areas of need.

65 What is Animal Assisted Therapy?

For the traditional community of professionals who have worked with and researched ASD, nontraditional treatment methods such as Animal Assisted Therapies may be hard to accept. There are no controlled research studies in which Animal Assisted Therapies are scientifically supported for the ASD population. However, some people report that positive changes have occurred for some of the people who have participated in the therapy. No one has claimed that animal assisted therapies is a "cure" for ASD, nor does the community who support Animal Assisted Therapies even know for certain why it can have a positive effect on some individuals. They hypothesize that it may be the sensory input from the animals, the motor stimulation of the activities, the social contact with unconditional acceptance, or any number of other reasons. This type of therapeutic intervention is usually considered complementary to other, more traditional, forms of therapy, such as early intervention and education.

Therapeutic riding on horses is called Hippotherapy. The North American Riding for the Handicapped Association (NARHA) is the governing body that assesses and certifies instructors as well as qualifying centers for doing Hippotherapy. Therapeutic swimming with dolphins is called Dolphin Assisted Therapy.

Although not considered a therapy, dogs have also been used to assist individuals with ASD as well as individuals with other special needs. Most people have heard of "seeing-eye dogs" to help individuals who are blind, but dogs can also be helpful in many other ways. These dogs are typically called "service dogs." They can help alert an individual to an impending seizure; alert caregivers to problems; help in completing sequential and routine tasks; and they can facilitate positive social interaction and develop a sense of companionship.

66 What is Music Therapy?

Music Therapy was first introduced in the United States as a therapeutic intervention for war veterans in the 1940s. Since that time, it has expanded considerably and been used as a rehabilitation tool for various medical disabilities in populations ranging from preschoolers to geriatrics. Music Therapy continues to broaden its reach and relevancy in other contexts, such as musically assisted childbirth, rehabilitation and stress reduction.

With the ASD population, music is used as the vehicle or tool to try to connect with and expand an individual's communication skills, social abilities and behavior. It is common for individuals with ASD to have an interest in music and art; both considered "right brain activities." Music Therapy is tailored to the individual's unique needs. For some who may be severely impaired and not seemingly connected to the outside world, the goal of Music Therapy may simply be the initial connection with someone else. This can be seen when a music therapist uses a child's self-stimulating behaviors (e.g., rocking, hand flapping, jumping) as a means to match the child in his or her own world with the beat of the music. Then slowly changing the rhythm can implement a change in the child's behavior. Or, for a higher functioning child who has some vocabulary but does not use it effectively or socially, he or she may find the value of communication by learning to ask for a favorite song or permission to play a musical instrument.

The goals of Music Therapy are not to teach individuals how to play or make music. Rather, they are to expand a child's behavioral repertoire, increase social and communication skills, enhance motor control, increase feelings of self worth, and increase participation in constructive activities.

67 What is Vision Therapy?

Vision Therapy is a rehabilitative therapy shown to be effective in the treatment of binocular vision impairments and visual perceptual deficits. This includes conditions such as strabismus (being cross-eyed) and amblyopia (lazy eye). The core feature of Vision Therapy is to get the brain and eyes working together so that the information coming in from the eyes is accurately perceived and interpreted by the brain. This eye-brain process is presumed to be deficient in many individuals with ASD, but research has yet to support these approaches as efficacious with ASD individuals.

Vision Therapy consists of specific exercises and activities that can address the organization of visual space, visual attention, efficient eye teaming (coordination), depth perception, and improving one's ease and efficiency of visual processing. The exercises are either supervised by or administered by a medical professional with experience in vision therapy. This is typically an optometrist (OD), but can also be an opthamologist (MD).

Many individuals with ASD have visual difficulties involving such problems as difficulty utilizing peripheral vision, tunnel vision and hypersensitivity to lights. Light sensitivity (scotopic sensitivity) is typically triggered by various light sources and conditions. The Irlen Lens System was developed to help with light sensitivity. It involves using colored transparencies or overlays on written material in order to reduce visual perceptual stress. The benefits attributed to the method have been primarily anecdotal. Thus, this approach is controversial.

68 What diets are used to treat ASD individuals?

When people refer to a diet for individuals with ASD, they are usually referring to the gluten and casein free diets (GF/CF). Gluten and casein are proteins. They are found in many of the most common foods we eat, especially processed foods. Gluten is found in grains such as wheat, barley, oats and rye. Casein is a protein found in milk and diary products. It has been theorized that some forms of Autism may be due to the poor or incomplete breakdown of peptides that come from foods that contain gluten and casein and the excessive absorption of these peptides due to a "Leaky Gut" (see question 43). This theory has also been referred to as the "Opioid Excess Theory" of Autism because of the observation by a scientist named Jaak Pankseep in 1980 that Autistic children had many traits in common with people addicted to opioid drugs (see question 33). Therefore, eliminating gluten and casein from the diets of Autistic individuals has been suggested as a means to prevent further neurological and gastrointestinal damage, possibly generating a reduction in Autistic symptoms. Some proponents claim that the earlier the diet is implemented, the better the results in terms of symptom remission. At this time, there is no scientifically validated evidence for this approach; only anecdotal reports and unpublished studies.

Because of the high level of interest from many parents in these diets, there are numerous sources for gaining information as to why, and recipes for how, a child's diet can be made gluten and casein free. Some resources are provided in question 81.

Another dietary approach used with some individuals, specifically those with difficult to control seizures and those with a diagnosis of Landau-Kleffner, is called the ketogenic diet. This is a high fat diet and is considered more of a medical regime than a diet that must be followed exactly in order for it to be effective in controlling seizures. It is often a second line approach to seizure management when medications have not been effective. Often the diet is supplemented with vitamins, minerals and enzymes because of the inability of the diet to meet the nutritional needs of an individual, and also to break down the diet's high fat content. This is a very difficult diet and should be conducted under the supervision of a physician and nutritionist.

69 What vitamins and nutritional supplements are used with ASD individuals?

Nutritional supplements tend to fall into a general category of "natural alternatives" that often collide with traditional approaches, thereby being controversial. As with all approaches, you must be a critical thinker and investigate whether any particular approach might be beneficial in your particular case by considering all the available information. For the purposes of this book, a brief explanation about the more popular supplements that are commonly being used with individuals with ASD will be provided.

There are several studies that have examined how Autistic individuals absorb nutrients and whether there are nutritional deficiencies associated with ASD. Results of these studies suggest that some individuals with ASD have absorption problems resulting in chronic diarrhea or chronic constipation and/or they may have intestinal inflammations. Low levels of various vitamins and minerals have also been found in several studies examining the ASD population. There have also been studies linking Autism and poor immune system functioning or immune deficiencies. Proponents of so-called "alternative" approaches suggest that by supplementing the nutritional system with various vitamins and minerals, symptom reduction or elimination may be possible. At the very least, proponents believe that using supplements can enhance a child's gastrointestinal system, perhaps making them more amenable to other interventions.

Some of the supplements currently being used include:

- vitamin B6 and magnesium

- vitamin B12

- thiamin

- vitamin C

- vitamin A

- vitamin E

- cod liver oil

- essential fatty acids (omega-3 and omega-6)

- zinc

- glyconutrients and phytonutrients.

The most accurate measure of vitamin and mineral levels is through a blood test. Working with a knowledgeable physician is important not only to order the tests but also because, using supplements, often thought of as harmlessly "natural," is not without risks. Some can be toxic to the system, depending upon dosage and potential interactions with other agents. Copper is a mineral often found at unusually high levels in Autistic children and therefore probably should not be contained in dietary supplements.

A physician and/or a nutritionist should be consulted to guide you through the maze of nutritional supplements and to monitor any changes. Once particular supplements are chosen, careful and controlled monitoring over several weeks is often necessary to determine whether there have been any benefits.

70   What is Immunotherapy?

Immunotherapy is a treatment approach in which the immune system is targeted for enhancement. This is most commonly done by giving intravenous immunoglobulin G. This approach is based upon the premise that Autistic children have an autoimmune disorder in which the body is attacking itself. Autoimmune disease may be triggered by infections, viral or bacterial, and treatment protocols are often difficult to determine. Additionally, studies that have shown some benefit to Autistic children do not make it clear as to who might benefit from such intervention. Whether the benefit is limited to children with chronic infections or other immune deficiencies is not yet known. Ongoing research in this area is being conducted.

71   What medications are used to treat ASD?

There are no specific medications designed to either treat or cure ASD. The medications commonly used are for symptom management only. Therefore some individuals with ASD are not taking any medications, while others take several. The studies on the use of drugs for children and the ASD population are increasing, but most of the drugs prescribed have not yet been approved for use with children or specifically for the ASD population. The decision to take or not take medications to alleviate various symptoms is a decision between individuals and their physicians.

The medications prescribed for individuals with ASD are used for specific symptom management, such as attention and behavior. Therefore, the same drugs prescribed to treat the attentional issues of children with ADD or ADHD are used with ASD children. Similarly, drugs used to treat maladaptive behaviors, such as self-injurious behaviors and temper tantrums, have been used with depressed, anxious or psychotic patients.

Many of the current medications that are used to treat anxiety and depression, called Selective Serotonin Reuptake Inhibitors (SSRIs), are used with the ASD population for management of behavior. These drugs include Fluoxetine (Prozac), Fluvoxamine (Luvox), Sertraline (Zoloft), Paroxetine (Paxil) and Citalopram (Celexa). SSRIs may help reduce agitation, aggression, and increase an overall tolerance for changes, according to some studies.

Another group of drugs, referred to as neuroleptics or anti-psychotic drugs, has also been used in the ASD population to reduce agitation, aggression and repetitive behaviors. Drugs such as Chlorpromazine (Thorazine), Theoridazine (Mellaril) and Haloperidol (Haldol) are strong and can produce severe and possibly permanent neurological side effects. Therefore, their use is typically for a temporary reduction in the problem behaviors rather than long-term use.

There is a newer group of drugs, the atypical neuroleptics, which have fewer side effects than the neuroleptics. This group includes such medications as Clozapine (Clozaril), Olanzapine (Zyprexa), Risperidone (Risperdal), Quetiapine (Seroquel) and Ziprasidone (Zeldox).

Other medications have been used with ASD populations that are too numerous to mention here. A list of medications in Appendix F includes some of the drugs described here, and additional information about them. This is not a comprehensive list of every drug available. And, with new drugs still in development, more options will likely be available in the future.

72   How is Melatonin used in treating ASD?

Melatonin is a hormone produced in the body that helps regulate the sleep-wake cycle. It has been used with the ASD population in an effort to develop a better sleep cycle because of their reported sleep difficulties. While sleep adjustments won't cure ASD, a well-rested individual can show overall improvement in his or her functioning during the wake cycle, not to mention the benefits to the parents and other family members who might actually get a decent night's sleep themselves!

Some studies involving Melatonin have documented improvements in the sleep cycles of up to 80% of Autistic individuals. For some, the effects wear off over time. Research in the ASD population is continuing in this area to determine exactly why and how the melatonin works so people can better determine how to administer it and in what doses. Melatonin is considered a natural hormone but, too often, people assume that because something is a natural supplement or something naturally produced in the body, there are no associated risks. This is simply an incorrect assumption and caution is urged in taking Melatonin – or anything else.

73   Are there specific interventions for toilet training?

Most approaches to toilet training are behaviorally based interventions. They are generally employed along with providing an understanding of the sensory and communicative functions associated with the toileting experience. There are sensory components, such as recognizing the need to release oneself, the awareness of how exactly to do that, and the language to express to another person that a diaper is full or there is a need to go sit on the toilet.

The number of books and resources on this topic is substantial. Several resources are provided in question 81 to help begin your search for the information that may be most relevant to your particular situation.

74   Are there specific interventions for temper tantrums?

Temper tantrums are one of the most difficult, frustrating and potentially embarrassing aspects of ASD. Few parents have escaped the public display from a child who will not respond to either words or actions, appears inconsolable, and is engaging in the type of ear piercing screams that suggest you're cruelly inflicting the worst of all pains. Generally, behavioral approaches have been found to be the most effective in addressing temper tantrums.

The types of possible interventions can be as unique as the individuals experiencing the tantrums. Most important for parents to understand is that the temper tantrum is a means of communication. It's not one that is acceptable, but is nonetheless a form of communication. Therefore, attempting to understand the reason for the tantrum can be important in determining how best to intervene. Observational skills are critical, and doing a functional analysis of behavior (detailed observation and recording of events surrounding the episode) can be invaluable in alerting you to what the behavior possibly means and what you can do about it.

Knowing when to simply ignore behaviors, when to reason and explain with the child, when to adjust sensory experiences, or when to avoid certain contexts, are all critical in evaluating how to intervene in a particular temper tantrum for a particular individual. Utilizing visual schedules and visual prompts has been shown to be effective in helping some individuals better understand changes in their routine or simply understand what to expect, in order to decrease many temper tantrums that can result from the fear of the unknown and unexpected changes in routines.

75 Are there specific interventions for social skills deficits?

Social skills deficits are one of the core features of ASD. The extent to which an individual's social competence can be impaired varies considerably across people. There are some individuals who are totally isolated and withdraw from all social contexts, others who tolerate simple interactions and may learn basic skills, and still others wish to engage socially but do not have the necessary skills to be successful. The types of interventions are therefore going to be different for each of these populations.

The development of social skills includes such factors as communication including body language, spatial issues (how physically close to be to others), facial expressions; play skills, turn-taking skills; recognizing, responding to and expressing emotions, initiating, maintaining and terminating interactions; perspective taking and understanding motives; as well as the development of higher-level cognitive skills, including problem solving and reasoning, to name just some of the skills necessary to be socially competent.

Social skills are at the core of communicative competence. In other words, we learn to communicate in order to engage with others in social contexts. In the speech-language profession, this is called pragmatic language, and speech-language pathologists are the primary professionals who address this area of development. In working with the ASD population, you may find speech-language pathologists, psychologists and behaviorists or autism "specialists" or "trainers" who work with social skills deficits. Other professionals working with ASD individuals may find that their work will also benefit an individual's social development.

Initially bringing a person "out of his or her shell" is a goal for many lower functioning individuals who attempt to remove themselves from their surroundings and the people in them. There are a number of interventions that have been used for this goal, and the research most supports behavioral based approaches. Some will follow the child's lead and match their behavior in order to gain a connection before attempting to move them out of their own world and into "ours." Others will direct the child and reinforce certain desired behaviors such as eye contact.

For those individuals with some basic communicative skills, one of the goals of social skills training is to develop their pragmatic language skills in a way that expands the functions of their language. For many of these individuals, they may use only single words or just a few words to get their basic needs met (e.g., cookie, go to McDonalds), or they may repeat a TV program jingle to indicate they want to watch that program. But, they don't use their language for other purposes beyond "I want (whatever)." For these individuals, teaching them the vocabulary they need to expand the functions of their language is necessary. Teaching them to point and engage in shared attention, to take turns in basic exchanges and to ask questions are all types of skills necessary to have as basic social skills. Whether this is developed as a spontaneous skill or remains rote or a scripted experience depends upon the functional level of the individual.

Typically, play skills naturally go together with teaching communication in the activities that are chosen to develop social skills. Play skills begin with initially understanding how to use toys. Many children do not know that a ball is for rolling/throwing, a block is for building and a doll is for dressing or feeding. Developing the skills for what to do with toys is necessary before expecting an individual to play appropriately with others.

For the higher level individuals whose language may be fairly well developed but their proficiency of relating to others is impaired or awkward, language therapy and cognitive-behavioral therapy are generally effective. A variety of different techniques and strategies is used in these therapies, including role playing, use of video feedback, watching and interpreting social contexts in TV and movies, social stories and comic strip conversations (described below) to name just a few.

Carol Gray developed two techniques that have become widely accepted in working on social skills development: "Social Stories" and "Comic Strip Conversations". Social Stories essentially provide a written story of a social context to help individuals understand their personal role in the interaction, what they are doing and need to do, and the perspective of others in the interaction. Stories range from very simple to complex depending upon the needs of the individual. Carol has written several books demonstrating Social Stories and describing how they are to be written (see references below). Comic Strip Conversations are a vehicle for visually seeing the thoughts and feelings of individuals in an interaction through the use of comic strips that visually represent thoughts in "thought bubbles" and speech in "speech bubbles." Colors are added to the comic strip to represent emotions in the context.

Various supplements and medications have demonstrated their usefulness in increasing social interaction in some individuals. Although they do not facilitate proficiency in social skills, they have been noted to make an individual more responsive and available to social contexts and therefore more likely to benefit from the other therapies offered.

76 Are there specific interventions for sleep disturbances?

Approximately 40–70% of ASD children have sleep disturbances. When a child doesn't get enough sleep, it often means that parents and other family members are also sleep deprived. Thus, not only the ASD individual is affected by sleep problems. The types of intervention described here are not unique to ASD individuals, but how they are implemented (i.e., visual schedules, pictures) may need to be adapted according to individual needs.

There are two primary avenues for addressing sleep disturbances: behavioral/environmental and medical. First, it is helpful to get an accurate assessment of what the exact problem is within the sleep cycle. Is it difficulty in initially falling asleep, staying asleep or waking earlier than necessary? Keeping a record of the situations surrounding bedtime can be invaluable in looking for patterns and identifying specific areas for intervention. Observe when the child goes to sleep, circumstances around the bedtime, how long the child sleeps, if he or she wakes up, for how long, etc. This will be a starting point from which to discuss with your health care professional or caseworker how to proceed.

First, environmental and behavior changes should be considered. It is important to regulate the sleep environment. This means getting a bedtime routine, including a consistent and specific time and location for sleep. Avoid high activity levels or eating/drinking too much before bed. Avoid anxiety-provoking situations before bed, such as watching a scary movie or reading a scary story. Avoid daytime naps. Avoid snacks at night. Make the sleeping environment dark, cool and quiet.

Many parents believe it is necessary or desirable for them to lie down with their child in order for him or her to fall asleep. The mistake in this thinking is that the child comes to associate that parent with sleep. When the parent is no longer there, and the child awakens, the whole process must be repeated.

Sleep disturbances can be either caused or exacerbated by a number of different medical conditions. For example, if a child has allergies or has a cold, an ear infection or is congested, has gastrointestinal problems and tummy aches, or is having seizures, these can lead to difficulties falling or staying asleep. In addition, if there are disturbances in the brain's regulation of the sleep-wake cycle (circadian rhythms), this will also have an effect on sleep patterns.

Various medications have been used with some success in treating sleep disturbances. Sometimes, over-the-counter antihistamines are used, or the hormone Melatonin. More often, prescription medications are used that are actually designed for other purposes: anti-depression medications, blood pressure medications and mood stabilizing medications. Whether or not medications are appropriate and which ones might be helpful is something to be discussed on an individual basis with your physician.

77   Are there specific interventions for self-injurious behaviors?

There are numerous types of self-injurious behaviors. Some of the more common behaviors include head banging, biting, hitting and scratching oneself. Approximately 5–17% of individuals diagnosed with Autism or Mental Retardation engage in self-injurious behaviors.

As with any intervention, what works for one individual may not work with another. This can be especially true with self-injurious behaviors (SIB) because of the underlying idiosyncratic reason for the behavior. In other words, if two ASD individuals both bang their hands to their heads, but one is doing it against their ear because of an ear infection and the other is doing it to try and stimulate sensation as a repetitive, self-stimulating behavior, then the interventions for what appear to be the same behavior will need to be different.

Traditionally, behavioral approaches have most often been used to treat individuals engaging in self-injurious behaviors. However, it is important to understand the reason why a behavior is occurring because it can have a significant impact on what type of intervention will be most beneficial. There are several theories as to why ASD individuals engage in self-injurious behaviors. They include frustration; a form of self-stimulating behavior to increase sensory stimulation; the fact that the behavior is pleasurable as a result of an increase in a brain chemical (endorphins); and the possibility that it is due to sub-clinical seizures. In addition, some theorists believe that there is also a social component for some individuals who engage in self-injurious behaviors such as attention seeking or task avoidance.

If an individual is engaging in self-injurious behaviors out of frustration, then approaches that can decrease the frustration and arousal are recommended. These may include Speech-Language Therapy to facilitate communication skills, relaxation exercises and sensory experiences to reduce the agitation, and behavioral approaches rewarding more appropriate calming activities.

For those individuals for whom self-injurious behaviors are considered to be part of a self-stimulating ritual behavior in which the person is seeking out some type of sensation, then sensory activities can be taught to gain similar sensations through more appropriate behaviors. Simple changes can lead to profound changes, but "thinking outside the box" is usually necessary. What about chewing gum instead of the inside of one's cheek or tongue?

Some research has studied how the release of endorphins, the brain's natural opiate-like painkillers, can create a pleasurable experience, which may happen when some individuals engage in self-injurious behaviors. It seems counterintuitive to think that harming oneself can be pleasurable. But if the brain releases a chemical that tells the cells in your body "this is pleasurable" then continuing to do it makes peculiar sense. This idea has led to the use of a medication called Naltrexone, which is a beta-endorphin inhibitor. It essentially blocks the release of the endorphin, and has resulted in a reduction or elimination of the self-injurious behavior in some individuals. Another medication that has shown to be successful for some individuals exhibiting self-injurious behaviors is called Risperidone.

Sub-clinical seizures can also lead to self-injurious behaviors. These seizures aren't readily observable, but are detected by abnormal EEG findings. Therefore, having an EEG to determine if seizures may be at the root of these behaviors is an important diagnostic step. If seizures are the cause, anti-convulsant medications can be considered a viable intervention.

For those individuals who engage in self-injurious behaviors to gain attention or avoid tasks, behavioral approaches may be effective, especially when used in conjunction with some of the other interventions described above.

Usually, the best way to take an educated guess about the underlying cause is to observe the individual. Look for *what* behavior is exhibited in *what* conditions. Look for *when* it occurs, such as time of day, during certain tasks, or when there's a change in the environment, e.g., when an individual is touched, a sound is presented or a light turned on or off. Look at *where* the behavior occurs – in a particular location? home? school? in the community? Look at *who* may be present during these self-injurious behaviors to determine what potential role they may play in the process.

It may or may not be possible to know for sure why the behavior is occurring. It may not even be possible to completely stop all self-injurious behaviors. The priority is keeping the individual safe from harm. Removing the person from certain environments, removing dangerous objects in the environment, locking doors and cabinets, and obtaining helmets or other protective devices are all potentially helpful in the quest for this individual's safety.

78 Are there specific interventions for auditory processing problems?

Yes. First, it is important to recognize that there are different kinds of auditory processing problems. For example, there can be deficits in sound discrimination (recognizing whether one sound is the same or different from another); figure-ground problems in which an individual has difficulty sorting out the important auditory information from the background noise (such as when a student is listening to a teacher amidst other students' chatter); problems sequencing sounds in order to blend them into a word, for example "c-a-t" makes "cat;" and auditory memory problems, to name just a few.

Approaches for treating auditory processing problems vary considerably according to the type of problem. Some approaches work directly on the auditory area (repeating sound patterns, deciphering sound similarities and differences, rhyming and blending tasks, etc.) while others consider addressing brain integration techniques by using whole body exercises and facilitating the crossover between the two hemispheres (activities that encourage using the right hand and foot on the left side of the body and vice versa, jumping, hopping and ball tossing while reciting linguistic information). Some recent approaches have begun to use a metronome to specifically address sequencing issues but these approaches have not yet had scientific research to support their work objectively.

Two computer programs have addressed the auditory processing difficulties experienced by many individuals with ASD: *FastForWord* and *Earobics*. Although these programs were initially designed for individuals with specific language impairments, their effectiveness for individuals with ASD has also been noticed since individuals with ASD have the kinds of auditory and language-processing deficits targeted in these programs. *FastForWord* is a trademarked name developed by Scientific Learning Corporation in California. This program slows speech sounds down and clarifies the sounds until the individual learns to recognize the subtle sound discriminations in speech. The program is run through the Internet with the capacity to adjust itself to the individual responses of the participant. The speech production is gradually increased as the individual's performance on the various computer "games" indicates such an increase is warranted. *FastForWord* is only available through trained practitioners and facilities (e.g., some school districts, clinics and hospitals) in the United States. It involves approximately an hour and a half a day of training for six weeks. There is substantial research on the *FastForWord* program supporting its effectiveness in addressing language-based processing deficits.

Earobics is less rigid than *FastForWord*, but does not have the same amount of research to support it. It is designed to promote literacy skills and has outcome reports from several sources documenting its efficacy in this area. It also consists of "playing" computer games that are designed to address the auditory processing deficits seen in children with language-learning impairments. It does so by working on the areas of speech sound discrimination, word discrimination, rhythm and rhyming. It does not require any specialized training to implement and does not have a specified period of time in which programs need to be completed.

PART 5

Resources/ Organizations/ Websites

79. What organizations are available for ASD individuals and their families?

80. What publications are available for ASD individuals and their families?

81. What other resources, websites and books are available for ASD individuals and their families?

82. What websites are available to provide therapy tools, learning activities and materials for working with ASD individuals?

This final section contains resources for further investigation into the various areas discussed in this book that may be of interest to you. The amount of information on ASD is rapidly expanding and these resources will be a starting place for most readers to access that information. I have visited many websites and read many articles and books on the subject of ASD, but I do not claim to have personal knowledge of all the information made available through these resources. This information is provided as a resource and is not intended to be considered an endorsement by this author for any of the products, sites or information presented. As I have advised throughout this book, be a good consumer and think critically about the information you are presented with and then use the professionals you trust to do a reality check before proceeding with any treatment interventions.

79 What organizations are available for ASD individuals and their families?

The following is a brief list of highly visible organizations that readers may find helpful. Each one can serve as a resource for additional information such as links to other sites of interest or to organizations that may be specific to where you live.

Asperger's Syndrome Education Network of America, Inc (ASPEN)
P.O. Box 2577
Jacksonville, FL 32202-2577
USA
Phone: 904-745-6741
www.asperger.org

Asperger's Syndrome Support Group (Inc)
P.O. Box 1427 Bibra Lake
Western Australia 6965
Phone: (61) 08-9472-1598
e-mail: assg@telstra.com

Asperger's Syndrome Support Network
P.O. Box 123
Lawnton, QLD 4501
Australia
Phone: 617-3285-7001

Autism Association of New South Wales
P.O. Box 361
Forestville, NSW 2087
Phone: 02-9452-5088
Fax: 02-9451-3447
www.autismas.com.au

Autistic Association of New Zealand
P.O. Box 7305
Sydenham, Christchurch
New Zealand
Phone: 03-332-1038

Autism Association of Western Australia
Phone: (61) 08-9489 8900
e-mail: autismwa.autism.org.au

Autism Association Queensland Inc
P.O. Box 363
Sunnybank QLD 4109
Australia
Phone: 617-3273-0000

Autism Europe
Avenue E. Van Beccelaere 26b, Bte.21
B-1170 Bruxelles, Belgium
Phone: 32-(0) 2 675-7505
Fax: 32 (0) 2 675-7270
www.autismeurope.arc.be

Autism National Committee (AUTCOM)
7 Teresa Circle
Arlington, MA 02174
USA

Autism Network International (ANI)
An independent organization run by individuals with
autism/PDD.
P.O. Box 448
Syracuse, NY 13210-0448
USA
Contact: Jim Sinclair

Autism Research Institute
4182 Adams Avenue
San Diego, CA. 92116
USA
www.autismresearchinstitute.com

Autism Research Unit
Sunderland University
School of Sciences (Health)
University of Sunderland
Sunderland SR2 7EE
UK
UK Tel: 0191 510 8922
osiris.sunderland.ac.uk/autism/index.html

Autism Societies and Chapters around the World
www.isn.net/~jypsy/autsoc.htm

Autism Society of America
7910 Woodmont Ave, suite 650
Bethesda, MD 20814-3015
USA
Phone: 301-657-0881 or 800-3AUTISM
Fax: 301-657-0869
Fax on demand for information: 800-329-0899 (in the US only)
www.autism-society.org/

Autism Victoria
P.O. Box 235
Ashburton, Victoria 3147
Australia
Phone: 03-9885-0533
Fax: 03-9885-0508
avoca.vicnet.net./au/~autism

Autism West Midlands
18 Highfield Road
Edgbaston
Birmingham B15 3DU
UK
www.autistismwestmidlands.org.uk

Irish Society for Autism
Unity Building
16/17 Lower O'Connell Street
Dublin 1, Republic of Ireland
Phone: 071-744684
Fax: 071-744224
osiris.sunderland.ac.uk/autism/irish.html

Parents and Professionals and Autism (PAPA) Resource Center
Knockbracken Healthcare Park
Saintfield Road
Belfast BT8 8BH
Northern Ireland
UK
www.autismni.org

The Center for Autism and Related Disorders (CARD)
Various locations throughout the United States
www.centreforautism.com

The National Autistic Society (UK)
393 City Road
London EC1V 1NE
Phone: 020-7833-2299
Fax: 020-7833-9666
www.oneworld.org/autism-uk

World Autism Organisation (WAO)
Contact c/o **Autism Europe**

80 What publications are available for ASD individuals and their families?

In addition to the organizations and websites identified in this section, there are several newsletters and magazines that can be very helpful to individuals and their families. There are also a number of professional journals. This list is by no means exhaustive. Phone numbers that have an area code of "800" are free numbers in the United States. They cannot be called from outside the US.

Newsletters/Magazines

The Advocate
Published by the Autism Society of America six times a year.
Members of ASA receive *The Advocate* as part of their membership.

7910 Woodmont Ave, Suite 300
Bethesda, MD 20814-3067
USA
Phone: 301-657-0881 or 800-3AUTISM
Fax: 301-657-0869
Fax on demand for information: 800-329-0899
www.autism-society.org

The ANDI News
Quarterly newsletter published by the Autism Network for
Dietary Intervention.

P.O. Box 335
Penninton, NJ 08534-0335
www.autismNDI.com

Asperger United
Quarterly newsletter published by The National Autistic Society
in the UK.

393 City Road
London EC1V 1NG
Phone: 020-7903-3542
Fax: 020-7903-3767

Autism-Asperger's Digest Magazine
Published bimonthly by Future Horizons, Inc

721 W. Abram Street
Arlington, TX 76013
USA
Phone: 817-277-0727 or 800-489-0727
Fax: 817-277-2270
www.autismdigest.com

Autism In Focus Online Newsletter
1900 K Street SW
Cedar Rapids, Iowa 52404
USA
Phone: 319-364-2687
www.autismawakeninginia.bizland.com

Autism Research Review International
Published quarterly by the Autism Research Institute.

4182 Adams Avenue
San Diego, CA 92116
USA
Fax: 619-563-6840
www.autismresearchinstitute.com

National Autistic Society Newsletter
The National Autistic Society
393 City Road
London EC1V 1NG
UK
http://www.nas.org.uk

The Communicator
Newsletter published quarterly by the Autism National Committee
(AUTCOM).

7 Teresa Circle
Arlington, MA 02174
USA

Jenison Autism Journal: Creative Ideas in Practice
(formerly called The Morning News)
Published quarterly by the Jenison Public Schools in Grand
Rapids, Michigan and edited by Carol Gray.

Jenison High School, Jenison Autism Journal
2140 Bauer Rd
Jenison, MI 49428

Subscriptions from Australia should write to:

Mick Clark
Giant Steps Tasmania
35 West Church St
P.O. Box 300
Tasmania
Australia 7304

Subscriptions from New Zealand should write to:

Maree Whitworth
Autistic Association of New Zealand
P.O. Box 7
Sydenham, Christchurch
New Zealand

Subscribtions from the UK should write to:

Keith Lovett
Autism Independent (UK)
199/201 Blandford Abenue
Kettering
Northants NN16 9AT

Looking Up
International newsletter published monthly.

Editor: Adam Feinstein
P.O. Box 25727
London SW19 1WF
UK
Phone/fax: 020-8542-7702
e-mail: LookingUp@compuserve.com
www.feinst.demon.co.uk/looking-up.html

Our Voice
Newsletter published by the Autism Network International (ANI).

P.O. Box 448
Syracuse, NY 13210-0448
USA
Contact: Jim Sinclair

Professional Journals

Autism: The International Journal of Research and Practice
Published four times a year by SAGE Publications in association
with The National Autistic Society in the UK.

Journals Subscription manager, SAGE Publications Ltd
6 Bonhill St
London EC 2A 4PU
UK
Fax: 020-7374-8741

Focus on Autism and Other Developmental Disabilities
Published quarterly by PRO-ED, Inc

8700 Shoal Creek Blvd
Austin, TX 78757
USA
Phone: 512 451-3246 or 800-897-3202
Fax: 800-FXPROED
www.proedinc.com

Good Autism Practice
Published twice a year by the British Institute of Learning
Disabilities (BILD).

BILD
Campion House
Green Street
Kidderminster
Worcs
DY10 1JL
UK
Subscriptions administrator: Marie Davis
(E-mail m.davis@bild.org.uk)

Phone: 01562 723010
Fax: 01562 723029

The Journal of Applied Behavior Analysis (JABA)
Published quarterly by:

The Society for Experimental Analysis of Behavior, Inc
Department of Human Development, University of Kansas
1000 Sunnyside Avenue
Lawrence, KS 66045-2133
USA
Phone: 785-843-0008
www.envmed.rochester.edu/wwwrap/behavior/jaba/
jabahome.htm

Journal of Autism and Developmental Disorders
Published bimonthly by Kluwer Academic/Plenum Publishers.

Subscription inquiries: In North, South and Central America:

Kluwer Academic Publishers, Journals Dept.
101 Philip Drive
Assinippi Park
Norwell, MA 02061
USA

Phone: 781-871-6600
Fax: 781-681-9045
e-mail: kluwer@wkap.com

Subscriptions in all other countries:

Kluwer Academic Publishers, Journals Dept. Distribution
Centre
P.O. Box 322
3300 AH Dordrecht
The Netherlands
Phone: 31 78 6392392
e-mail: orderdept@wkap.nl

Technical Manuals

Diagnostic and Statistical Manual of Mental Disorders (4th edn)
    (1984). Washington, DC: American Psychiatric Association.
*International Statistical Classification of Diseases and Related Health
    Problems* (10th revision) (1992). Geneva, Switzerland: World
    Health Organization.

81 What other resources, websites and books are available for ASD individuals and their families?

The number of resources available to obtain information on
ASD both in print and on the web is constantly expanding. You
will find over 100 sites associated with ASD by simply typing
in www.autism.com (and that is just the beginning and not
even the name of an organization).

The following list of websites and books is provided
according to some of the common areas of interest. The list is
by no means exhaustive, but it does provide a basis for readers
to explore their interests. The first section provides general,

highly visible websites with good information – good places to begin. The rest of this section separates the resources according to general topic areas.

CAUTION: It is important to remember that there are no controls or monitoring system for what can be written on the internet and by whom. Please be a critical thinker, research your concerns and use professionals for support and additional information.

www.autism.com
Center for the Study of Autism – Links to all topics on ASD

www.autism.fm
Yale Child Study Center – Developmental Disabilities Clinic and Research Home Page

www.autism-india.org/worldwideorgs.html
Autism organizations worldwide

www.autismonline.org
Connecting parents with professionals around the world. Resources and links in over 20 languages.

www.autistics.org
A site primarily by and for people with Autism/AS.

www.autism-resources.com
Autism Resources

www.autism-society.org
Autism Society of America (ASA)

www.autismuk.com
Society for the Autisicially Handicapped (SFTAH) in the UK

www.canfoundation.org
Cure Autism Now (CAN)

www.cdc.gov/ncbddd/dd/ddautism.htm
The Center for Disease Control and Prevention (CDC)'s Autism Information Center

www.centerforautism.com
Center for Autism and Related Disorders (CARD)

www.inlv.demon.nl/internaut/
InternAUT – an international Autism self-advocacy organization

ireland.iol.ie/~wise/autinet/anflinks.htm
International site with many links including those for
non-English-speaking countries.

www.isn.net/~jypsy/autilink.htm
Oops Wrong Planet Syndrome

www.mindinstitute.com
The MIND Institute

www.naar.org
National Alliance for Autism Research (NAAR)

www.nimh.nih.gov/publicat/autism.cfm
National Institutes of Health NIMH Division

www.oneworld.org/autism-uk
The National Autistic Society

www.udel.edu/bkirby/asperger
Online Asperger Syndrome Information and Support (OASIS)

Allergies

Books

Rapp, D.J. (1992) *Is This Your Child? Discovering and Treating
Unrecognized Allergies in Children and Adults.* New York: William
Morrow & Co.

Websites

www.allergyconnection.com/layton
The Allergy Connection

www.autismresearchinstitute.com
The Autism Research Institute distributes an information packet on vitamins, allergies, and nutritional treatments for Autism.

www.autismmedical.com
Allergy induced Autism (AiA) is a group in the UK providing information on the connection between allergies and Autism.

Animal Assisted Therapies

Websites

www.assistance-dogs-intl.org
Assistance Dogs International, Inc

www.grandin.com/references/thinking.animals.html
Information from Temple Grandin's perspective.

www.iaadp.org
International Association of Assistance Dog Partners

www.narha.org/autism.html
The North American Riding for the Handicapped Association

www.rehabnet.com/aft/
An overview and bibliography of Animal-Facilitated Therapy.

www.tufts.edu/vet/cfa/aft_bib.html
Tufts Center for Animals and Public Policy

www.wolfpacks.com/serviced.htm
General information and a service dog directory.

Examples of organizations training service dogs and matching them with people who are disabled are:

www.nsd.on.ca/nsd/
National Service Dogs, New Hamburg, Ontario

Special Skills Dogs of Canada
P.O. Box 907
Oakville, Ontario, L6J 5E8
Canada
specializes in training seizure-alert dogs.

Art Therapy

Books

Evans, K. and Dubowski, J. (2001) *Art Therapy with Children on the Autistic Spectrum.* London: Jessica Kingsley Publishers.

Flowers, Tony (1996) *Reaching Children with Autism through Art: Practical Fun Activities to Enhance Motor Skills and to Improve Tactile and Concept Awareness.* Arlington, TX: Future Horizons.

Websites

www.arttherapy.org
The American Art Therapy Association

www.arttherapyincanada.ca
Art Therapy in Canada

www.baat.org/autism.htm
The British Association for Art Therapy

www.ctrf.net/asafari
ASAFARI Gallery of Autistic Spectrum Art

www.mmbmusic.com
Links to creative art and music sites

Asperger Syndrome

Books

Attwood, T. (1998) *Asperger's Syndrome: A Guide for Parents and Professionals.* London: Jessica Kingsley Publishers.

Cumine, V., Leach, J. and Stevenson, G. (1998) *Asperger Syndrome: A Practical Guide for Teachers.* London: David Fulton Publishers.

Jackson, L. (2002) *Freaks, Geeks and Asperger Syndrome: A User Guide to Adolescence.* London: Jessica Kingsley Publishers.

Klin, A., Volkmar, F.R. and Sparrow, S.S. (eds) (2000) *Asperger Syndrome.* New York: Guilford Press.

Moyes, R.A. (2002) *Addressing the Challenging Behaviour of Children with High-functioning Autism/Asperger Syndrome in the Classroom: A Guide for Teachers and Parents.* London: Jessica Kingsley Publishers.

Ozonoff, S., Dawson, G. and McPartland, J. (2002) *A Parent's Guide to Asperger Syndrome & High Functioning Autism: How to Meet the Challenges and Help your Child Thrive.* New York: Guilford Press.

Paradiz, V. (2002) *Elijah's Cup: A Family's Journey into the Community and Culture of High-functioning Autism and Asperger's Syndrome.* New York: Free Press.

Romanowski Bashe, P. (2001) *The OASIS Guide to Asperger Syndrome: Advice, Support, Insight and Inspiration.* Carmarthen, Wales: Crown Publishers.

Smith-Myles, B. and Simpson, R.L. (1998) *Asperger Syndrome: A Guide for Educators and Parents.* Austin, TX: PRO-ED.

Smith-Myles, B. and Southwick, J. (1999) *Asperger Syndrome and Difficult Moments: Practical Solutions for Tantrums, Rage, and Meltdowns.* Shawnee Mission, KS: Autism Asperger Publishing Co.

Stewart, K. (2002) *Helping a Child with Nonverbal Learning Disorder or Asperger's Syndrome.* Oakland, CA: New Harbinger Publications.

Websites

www.aspergers.com
Asperger's Disorder Homepage by R. Kaan Ozbayrak, M.D.

www.asperger.org/index_asc.html
Asperger Syndrome Coalition of the US

www.btinternet.com/~black.ice/addnet/aspergers.html
Asperger's Syndrome Information Sources

www.isn.net/~jypsy/autilink.htm
Oops Wrong Planet Syndrome

www.udel.edu/bkirby/asperger
Online Asperger Syndrome Information and Support (OASIS)

www.users.dircon.co.uk/~cns/index.html
Univeristy students with Autism and Asperger's Syndrome

Auditory Processing and Auditory Integration Training

Books

Kelly, D.A. (1995) *Central Auditory Processing Disorder: Strategies for Use with Children and Adolescents.* San Antonio, TX: Communication Skill Builders.

Madaule, P. (1993) *When Listening Comes Alive: A Guide to Effective Learning and Communication.* Norval, Ontario: Moulin Publishing.

Richard, G.J. (2001) *The Source for Processing Disorders.* East Moline, IL: LinguiSystems.

Informational Websites

www.ari.com
Autism Research Institute

www.autism-society.org/packages/auditory.html
Autism Society of America

www.georgianainstitute.org
The Georgiana Organization

www.ideatrainingcenter.com
Idea Training Center

www.listeningfitness.com
Listening Fitness Program

www.sait.org
The Society for Auditory Intervention Training

www.samonas.com
Samonas Auditory Intervention

www.seriouscomposer.com
Auditory Integration Training Center

www.tomatis.com
Tomatis Americas Network

Product Websites

www.crossroadsinstitute.org
Learning to Listen

www.earobics.com
Cognitive Concepts

www.interactivemetronome.com
Interactive Metronome Home Page

pages.cthome.net/cbristol/capd-pro.html
CAPD Remediation Programs and Materials

www.rmlearning.com
The Listening Program

www.scientificlearning.com
Scientific Learning Corporation

www.thelisteningprogram.net/autism
Advanced Brain Technologies

www.vision-audio.com
Electronic Audio Stimulation effect (EASe CD)

Augmentative Communication

Books

Beukelman, D.R. and Mirenda, P. (1998) *Augmentative and Alternative Communication*, 2nd edn, Baltimore, MD: Paul H. Brookes.

Bondy, A. and Frost, L. (1994) *The Picture Exchange Communication System*. Pyramid Educational Consultants.

Websites

www.augcominc.com
Augmentative Communication, Inc (ACI) publishes: *Augmentative Communications News* and *Alternatively Speaking*, distributed worldwide.

www.autism.net/html/bondy-frost.html
The Geneva Centre site

www.bconnex.nt/~randys/
Animated American Sign Language Dictionary

www.gallaudet.edu
Gallaudet University

www.handspeak.com
Self-instructive site for sign language with signs provided in animation.

www.isaac-online.org
International Association of Augmentative Communication

www.oise.utoronto.ca/~ortcpm/index.htm
Augmentative and Alternative Communication Advocacy Group

www.pecs.com
Picture Exchange Communication Symbols (PECS)

www.puzzlingthoughts.com
Canadian supplier of symbols and other learning materials.

www.signingtime.com
Teaches infants and toddlers to sign.

www.sign-lang.uni-hamburg.de/bibweb/
International Bibliography of Sign Language

Autism – general

Books

Frith, U. (ed) (1991) *Autism and Asperger Syndrome.* Cambridge University Press.

Hamilton, L.M. (2000) *Facing Autism: Giving Parents Reasons for Hope and Guidance for Help.* Colorado Springs, CO: Waterbrook Press.

Janzen, J.E. (1996) *Understanding the Nature of Autism: A Practical Guide.* San Antonio, TX: Therapy Skill Builders.

Marohn, S. (2002) *The Natural Medicine Guide to Autism.* Charlottesville, VA: Hampton Roads Publishing Co.

Richard, G.J. (2000) *The Source for Treatment Methodologies in Autism.* East Moline, IL: LinguiSystems.

Richard, G.J. (1997) *The Source for Autism.* East Moline, IL: LinguiSystems.

Schreibman, L. (1988) *Autism.* Newbury Park, CA: SAGE Publications, Inc.

Siegel, B. (1996) *The World of the Autistic Child: Understanding and Treating Autistic Spectrum Disorders.* New York: Oxford University Press.

Waltz, M. (1999) *Pervasive Developmental Disorders: Finding a Diagnosis and Getting Help.* Sebastopol, CA: O'Reilly & Associates, Inc.

Wing, L. (2001) *The Autistic Spectrum: A Parent's Guide to Understanding and Helping Your Child.* Berkeley, CA: Ulysses Press.

Autoimmune/Immune System Dysfunction

Books

Rapp, D. (1992) *Is This Your Child? Discovering and Treating Unrecognized Allergies in Children and Adults.* New York: Morrow & Co.

Websites

www.ari.com
Autism Research Institute – Dr. Bernard Rimland – Defeat Autism Now (DAN protocols)

www.neuroimmunedr.com
Dr Michael J. Goldberg and Neuro-Immune Dysfunction Syndromes (NIDS)

intramural.nimh.nih.gov/research/pdn/web.htm
National Institute of Mental Health study by Dr Susan Swedo on Pediatric Autoimmune Neuropsychiatric Disorder Associated with Streptococcus (PANDAS)

Behavior and Behavioral Approaches

Books

Fouse, E. and Wheeler, M. (1997) *A Treasure Chest of Behavioral Strategies for Individuals with Autism.* Arlington, TX: Future Horizons.

Harris, Sandra L. and Weiss, Mary (1998) *Right from the Start: Behavioral Intervention for Young Children with Autism: A Guide for Parents and Professionals.* Rockville, MD: Woodbine House.

Hodgdon, L.A. (1999) *Solving Behavior Problems in Autism: Improving Communication with Visual Strategies.* Troy, MI: QuirkRoberts Publishing.

Koegel, R.L., Rincover, A. and Egel, A.L. (1982) *Educating and Understanding Autistic Children.* San Diego, CA: College-Hill Press.

Lovaas. I. (2002) *Teaching Individuals with Developmental Delays: Basic Intervention Techniques.* Austin, TX: Pro-Ed.

Lovaas, I. (1981) *Teaching Developmentally Disabled Children: The ME Book.* Austin, TX: Pro-Ed.

Maurice, Catherine, Green, Gina and Luce, Stephen C. (1996) (eds) *Behavioral Intervention for Young Children with Autism.* Austin, TX: Pro-Ed.

McClannahan, L.E. and Krantz, P.J. (1999) *Activity Schedules for Children with Autism: Teaching Independent Behavior.* Bethesda, MD: Woodbine House.

Websites

icd.binghamton.edu
State University of New York, Institute for Child Development

rsaffran.tripod.com/aba.html
ABA Resources on the Internet

www.health.state.ny.us/nysdoh/eip/autism/ch4_pt2.htm
New York State Early Intervention Program Guidelines and Recommendations, Chapter 4 reprinted on the web

Communication

Books

Duke, M.P., Nowicki, S. and Martin, E.A. (1996) *Teaching Your Child the Language of Social Success.* Atlanta, GA: Peachtree Publishers Ltd

Freeman, S. and Dake, L. (1997) *Teach Me Language: A Language Manual for Children with Autism, Asperger's Syndrome and Related Developmental Disorders.* Langley, BC: SKF Books.

Gray, C. (2002) *My Social Stories Book.* London: Jessica Kingsley Publishers.

Gray, C. (1994) *The New Social Stories.* Arlington, TX: Future Horizons.

Gray, C. (1994) *Comic Strip Conversations.* Arlington, TX: Future Horizons.

Gray, C. (1993) *Taming the Recess Jungle.* Arlington, TX: Future Horizons.

Gutstein, S. (2001) *Autism/Aspergers; Solving the Relationship Puzzle.* Arlington, TX: Future Horizons.

Gutstein, S. and Sheely, R.K. (2002) *Relationship Development Intervention with Young Children – Social and Emotional Development Activities for Asperger Syndrome, Autism, PDD and NLD.* London: Jessica Kingsley Publishers.

Gutstein, S. and Sheely, R.K. (2002) *Relationship Development Intervention with Children, Adolescents and Adults – Social and Emotional Development Activities for Asperger Syndrome, Autism, PDD and NLD.* London: Jessica Kingsley Publishers.

Nowicki, S. and Duke, M. (1992) *Helping the Child Who Doesn't Fit In.* Atlanta, GA: Peachtree Publishers.

Quill, K.A. (2000) *Do-Watch-Listen-Say: Social and Communication Intervention for Children with Autism.* Baltimore: Brookes Publishing.

Shure, M. (1995) *Raising a Thinking Child Workbook.* New York: Henry Hold and Company.

Skillstreaming Series from Research Press (2612 N. Mattis Ave, Champaign IL 61821, Phone 800-519-2707)

Wetherby, A.M. and Prizant, B.M. (eds) (2000) *Autism Spectrum Disorder: A Transactional Developmental Perspective.* Baltimore, MD: Brookes Publishing.

Winner, M.G. (2003) *Thinking about You Thinking about Me.* London: Jessica Kingsley Publishers.

Winner, M.G. (2000) *Inside Out: What Makes a Person with Social-cognitive Deficits Tick?* London: Jessica Kingsley Publishers.

Websites

www.asha.org
American Speech-Language Hearing Association

www.comeunity.com
National Institute on Deafness and Other Communication Disorders

Diet

Informational and product websites for gluten/casein free diets

www.autismNDI.com
The Autism Network for Dietary Intervention (ANDI) (website in Spanish, French, German and Japanese)

www.autismresearchinstitute.com
The Autism Research Institute

www.eatright.org
American Dietetic Association

www.gfcfdietsupport.com *or* **www.gfcfdiet.com**
Diet information.

www.glutenfree.com
Foods and recipes.

www.glutino.com
Foods and recipes.

www.glutensolutions.com
Gluten-free groceries.

The Purine Research Society
5424 Beech Avenue
Bethesda, MD 20814-1730
Fax: 301-564-9597
For restricted purine diet e-mail: purine@erols.com.

For a copy of a restricted purine cookbook go to www.gout-haters.com.

Informational books and cookbooks for gluten/casein free diets

Fenster, C. (2002) *Wheat-Free Recipes & Menus: Delicious Dining Without Wheat or Gluten.* 4th edn. Centennial, CO: Savory Palate.

Fenster, C. (2001) *Special Diet Solutions: Healthy Cooking Without Wheat, Gluten, Dairy, Eggs, Yeast or Refined Sugar.* Centennial, CO: Savory Palate.

Fenster, C. (1999) *Special Diet Celebrations: No Wheat, Gluten, Dairy or Eggs.* Centennial, CO: Savory Palate.

Hagman, B. (2000) *The Gluten-Free Gourmet: Living Well Without Wheat.* New York: Owl Books.

Jackson, L (2002) *User Guide to the GF/CF Diet for Autism, Asperger Syndrome and AD/HD.* London: Jessica Kingsley Publishers.

Le Breton, M. (2002) *The Aia Gluten and Dairy Free Cookbook.* London: Jessica Kingsley Publishers.

Le Breton, M. (2001) *Diet Intervention and Autism: Implementing the Gluten Free and Casein Free Diet for Autistic Children and Adults.* London: Jessica Kingsley Publishers.

Lewis, L. (2001) *Special Diets for Special Kids Two.* Arlington, TX: Future Horizons.

Lewis, L. (1998) *Special Diets for Special Kids.* Arlington, TX: Future Horizons.

Sanderson, S. (2002) *Incredible Edible Gluten-Free Foods for Kids: 150 Family Tested Recipes.* Bethesda, MD: Woodbine House.

Seroussi, K. (2000) *Unraveling the Mystery of Autism and Pervasive Developmental Disorder: A Mother's Story of Research and Recovery.* New York: Simon & Schuster.

Enzymes (see also gastrointestinal and diet resources)

Books

DeFelice, K.L. (2002) *Enzymes for Autism and other Neurological Conditions: A Practical Guide.* Minneapolis, MN: Bang Printing.

Websites

www.groupsyahoo.com/group/enzymesandautism
Parent driven on-line forum.

Gastrointestinal issues (including Secretin)

Websites

www.AutismNDI.com
Autism Network for Dietary Intervention

www.autismresearchinstitute.com
The Autism Research Institute distributes an information packet on Celiac and casein sensitivity.

**curry.edschool.virginia.edu/go/cise/ose/information/
secretin.html**
John Wills Lloyds of the University of Virginia provides information and links on secretin.

www.secretin.com
An e-commerce site to order Victoria Beck's book 'Unlocking the Potential of Secretin', with additional links about secretin.

Genetic research information

Websites

www.agre.org
Autism Genetic Resource Exchange

www.autismgenes.org
Vanderbilt University Medical Center

www.autismgeneticresearch.org
Autism Genetic Research at New England Medical Center

www.autism-society.org
Autism Society of America (ASA)

www.chg.mc.duke.edu
Duke University Center for Human Genetics

www.exploringautism.org
A website exploring autism and genetics with links to articles and other resources.

www.naar.org
National Alliance for Autism Research (NAAR)

www.nhgri.nih.gov/index.html
National Human Genome Research Institute (NHGRI)

www.nichd.nih.gov/autism
National Institute of Child Heath and Development

www.nimh.nih.gov/publica/autism.cfm
National Institute of Mental Health (NIMH)

www.stanford.edu/group/cap/research/
Stanford University School of Medicine Dept of Psychiatry and Behavioral Sciences Autism Genetics Program

www.sutcliffelab.org
Vanderbilt University Medical Center

Health and the environment

Websites

www.amalgam.org
The dental amalgam issue.

www.autism.com/ari/mercury.html
Autism Research Institute

www.cdc.gov.nceh/lead/lead.htm
Center for Disease Control

www.doctorsdata.com
Doctor data reference laboratory

www.epa.gov
National Center for Environmental Research, US Environmental Protection Agency

www.extremehealthusa.com/mich.html
Extreme Health – Oral chelation and nutritional replacement therapy.

www.jorsm.com/~binstock
Teresa C. Binstock's research on immunological and infectious aspects of Autism Spectrum Disorders is recorded at this site.

www.mercury-k12.org
Mercury in Schools

www.mercvacalliance.com
Mervury Vaccine Alliance

www.niehs.nih.gov
National Institute of Environmental Health Sciences

www.preventingharm.org
Preventing harm is a resource and action center on children and the environment. It is not specific to the ASD population.

www.toxicteeth.net
Toxic Teeth organization

Immune system

Autism Autoimmunity Project
P.O. Box 293144
Davie, FL 33329
USA
Phone: 954-583-4860
FAX: 954-587-6509
www.gti.net/truegrit

Books

Seroussi, K. (2000) *Unraveling the Mystery of Autism and Pervasive Developmental Disorder: A Mother's Story of Research and Recovery.* New York: Simon & Schuster.

Medication

Books

Tsai, Luke (2001) *Taking the Mystery Out of Medications in Autism/Asperger Syndromes.* Arlington, TX: Future Horizons.

Websites

www.fda.gov/cder/drug/default.html
Food and Drug Administration – official US information

www.hc-sc-gc.ca/hpb-dgps/therapeut/htmleng/dpd.html
Canadian Drug Product Database

www.patientcenters.com/autism/news/med_reference.html
Autism Center–Patient Center Guides

Melatonin

Information and product websites

www.aveiveos.com/diet/melatonin
Aeiveos Research Library

www.gsdl.com
Great Smokies Diagnostic Laboratories

www.udaan.org/drugs/autrx2.html
UDAAN and Foundation for Spastic and Mentally Handicapped
Persons

Music Therapy

Books

Berger, D. (2002) *Music Therapy, Sensory Integration and the Autistic
     Child.* London: Jessica Kingsley Publishers.

Websites

www.geocities.com/Paris/Metro/8395
Music Therapy Around the World (website in English, Spanish
and Portuguese)

www.musictherapy.org
American Music Therapy Association website provides
information about Music Therapy in various countries around the
world.

www.musictherapyworld.net
World Federation for Music Therapy

Nonverbal Learning Disabilities

Books

Rourke, B. (1995) *Syndrome of Nonverbal Learning Disabilities: Neurodevelopmental Manifestations.* New York: Guilford Press.

Rourke, B. (1989) *Nonverbal Learning Disabilities: The Syndrome and the Model.* New York: Guilford Press.

Tanguay, P.B. (2002) *Nonverbal Learning Disabilities at School: Educating Students with NLD, Asperger, and Related Conditions.* London: Jessica Kingsley Publishers.

Thompson, S. (1997) *The Source for Nonverbal Learning Disorders.* East Moline, IL: LinguiSystems.

Whitney, R.V. (2002) *Bridging the Gap: Raising a Child with Nonverbal Learning Disorder.* New York: Berkley Publishing Group.

Websites

www.nldline.com
NLD information and links.

www.nldontheweb.org
NLD information and links.

Occupational Therapy

Books

Anderson, E. and Emmons, P. (1996) *Unlocking the Mysteries of Sensory Dysfunction: A Resource for Anyone who Works with, or Lives with a Child with Sensory Issues.* Arlington, TX: Future Horizons.

Ayres, J. (1979) *Sensory Integration and the Child.* Los Angeles: Western Psychological Services.

Kranowitz, C. (2003) *The Out of Sync Child has Fun: Activities for Kids with Sensory Integration Dysfunction.* New York: Perigee.

Kranowitz, C. (1998) *The Out of Sync Child: Recognizing and Coping with Sensory Integration Dysfunction.* New York: Perigee.

Kranowitz, C., Szklut, S., Balzer-Martin, L., Haber, E. and Sava, D.I. (2001) *Answers to Questions Teachers Ask About Sensory Integration.* Las Vegas, NV: Sensory Resources.

Myles, B.S., Cook, K.T., Miller, N.E., Rinner, L. and Robbins, L (2001) *Asperger Syndrome and Sensory Issues: Practical Solutions for Making Sense of the World.* Shawnee Mission, KS: Autism Asperger Publishing Co.

Schneider, Catherine Chemin (2001) *Sensory Secrets: How to Jump-start Learning in Children.* Lyman, SC: Concerned Communications.

Yack, E., Sutton, S. and Aquilla, P. (1998) *Building Bridges through Sensory Integration: Occupational Therapy for Children with Autism and Pervasive Developmental Disorder.* Toronto, Ontario: Parentbooks.

Websites

www.childrensdisabilities.info/sensory_integration/resources.html
Children's disabilities.

www.out-of-sync-child.com
Out of sync child book and resources.

www.sensoryint.com
Sensory Integration International The Ayers Clinic

www.sensorylearning.com
Sensory Learning Website

www.sensoryresources.com
Resource site.

www.sensory-dynamics.com
Sensory Dynamics Institute

www.sinetwork.org
Sensory Integration Network

www.wfot.org
World Federation of Occupational Therapists

Pivotal Response Therapy

www.psy.ucsd.edu/~vcestone/lab.html
University of California at San Diego Autism Research Laboratory

Rett Syndrome

International Rett Syndrome Association
9121 Piscataway Rd, Suite 2B
Clinton, MD 20735-2561
USA
Phone: 301-856-3334
www.rettsyndrome.org

Seizures and ketogenic diet resources

Books

Freeman, J.M., Millicent, T.K. and Freeman, J.B. (1996) *The Epilepsy Diet Treatment: An Introduction to The Ketogenic Diet.* 2nd edn, New York: Demos Medical Publishing.

Websites

www.epilepsy.org.uk
Epilepsy Action, previously called the British Epilepsy Association

www.growingstrong.org/epilepsy
Epilepsy resources.

www.ketogenic.org
Ketogenic Diet organization

www.stanford.edu/group/keodiet/
Stanford University

Organizations

The Charlie Foundation – to help cure Pediatric Epilepsy
1223 Wilshire Blvd 815
Santa Monica, CA 90403-5406
USA
Phone: 800-367-5386
e-mail: ketoman@aol.com

Epilepsy Foundation of America
Phone: 800-332-1000

MedicAlert
Phone (in the US): 800-432-5378 (to obtain medical alert bracelets)

Parents Helping Parents (PHP)
3041 Olcott Street
Santa Clara, CA 95054
USA
Phone: 408-727-5775

Keto Klub newsletter
Keto Klub
61557 Miami Meadows Court
South Bend, IN 46614
USA

Self-Injurious Behavior

Books

Schroeder, S.R., Oster-Granite, M.L. and Thompson, T. (2002) *Mental Retardation, Autism and Self-Injurious Behavior: Gene-brain-behavior relationships.* Washington, DC: American Psychological Association.

Websites

www.autismresearchinstitute.com
Autism Research Institute, information packet on SIB available

www.merrill.ku.edu/IntheKnow/sciencearticles/selfinjuri ousbehavior.html
University of Kansas-Merrill Advanced Studies Center

www.vanderbilt.edu/kennedy/topics/selfinj.htm
Research on SIB at Vanderbilt University

If you would like to obtain more information about Naltrexone as a medication in the treatment of SIB contact:
Dr. Jaak Panksepp
Department of Psychology
Bowling Green State University
Bowling Green, OH 43403-0228
USA

Sensory issues

Books

Anderson, E. and Emmons, P. (1996) *Unlocking the Mysteries of Sensory Dysfunction: A Resource for Anyone who Works with, or Lives with a Child with Sensory Issues.* Arlington, TX: Future Horizons.

Ayres, J. (1979) *Sensory Integration and the Child.* Los Angeles: Western Psychological Services.

Kranowitz, C. (2003) *The Out of Sync Child has Fun: Activities for Kids with Sensory Integration Dysfunction.* New York: Perigee.

Kranowitz, C. (1998) *The Out of Sync Child: Recognizing and Coping with Sensory Integration Dysfunction.* New York: Perigee.

Kranowitz, C., Szklut, S., Balzer-Martin, L., Haber, E. and Sava, D.I. (2001) *Answers to Questions Teachers Ask About Sensory Integration.* New York: Perigee.

Myles, B.S., Cook, K.T., Miller, N.E., Robbins, L.A. and Chiles, P. (2001) *Asperger Syndrome and Sensory Issues.* Shawnee Mission, KS: Autism Asperger Publishing Company.

Schneider, Catherine Chemin (2001) *Sensory Secrets: How to Jump-start Learning in Children*. Lyman, SC: Concerned Communications.

Yack, E., Sutton, S. and Aquilla, P. (1998) *Building Bridges through Sensory Integration: Occupational Therapy for Children with Autism and Pervasive Developmental Disorder*. Toronto, Ontario: Parenthoods.

Informational websites

www.childrensdisabilities.info/sensory_integration/resources.html
Children's disabilities.

www.out-of-sync-child.com
Out of sync child book and resources.

www.sensoryint.com
Sensory Integration International The Ayers Clinic

www.sensorylearning.com
Sensory Learning Website

www.sensoryresources.com
Resource site.

www.sensory-dynamics.com
Sensory Dynamics Institute

www.sinetwork.org
Sensory Integration Network

www.wcpt.org
World Confederation of Physical Therapy

www.wfot.org
World Federation of Occupational Therapists website

Product websites

www.flaghouse.com

www.intelisense.com

www.magicaltoysandproducts.com

www.sensorycomfort.com

www.SensoryResources.com

www.southpawenterprises.com

www.weightedvest.com

Siblings

Websites

www.chmc.org/departmt/sibsupp
Sibling Support Project

www.siblingsofautism.com
Written by a sibling about having an older brother with autism.

Sleep

Books

Durand, V.M. (1998) *Sleep Better! A Guide to Improving Sleep for Children with Special Needs.* Baltimore, MD: Paul H. Brookes.

Social skills information

Books

Duke, M.P., Nowicki, S. and Martin, E.A. (1996) *Teaching Your Child the Language of Social Success.* Atlanta, Georgia: Peachtree Publishers.

Gray, C. (1994) *The Social Story Book.* Arlington, TX: Future Horizons.

Gray, C. (1994) *Comic Strip Conversations.* Arlington, TX: Future Horizons.

Gray, C. (1993) *Taming the Recess Jungle.* Arlington, TX: Future Horizons.

Gray, C. and White, A.L. (2002) *My Social Stories Book*. London: Jessica Kingsley Publishers.

Gutstein, S. (2001) *Autism/Aspergers; Solving the Relationship Puzzle*. Arlington, TX: Future Horizons.

Gutstein, S. and Sheely, R.K. (2002) *Relationship Development Intervention with Young Children – Social and Emotional Development Activities for Asperger Syndrome, Autism, PDD and NLD*. London: Jessica Kingsley Publishers.

Gutstein, S. and Sheely, R.K. (2002) *Relationship Development Intervention with Children, Adolescents and Adults – Social and Emotional Development Activities for Asperger Syndrome, Autism, PDD and NLD*. London: Jessica Kingsley Publishers.

McAffe, J., MD (2002) *Navigating the Social World: A Curriculum for Individuals with Asperger's Syndrome, High Functioning Autism and Related Disorders*. Arlington, TX: Future Horizons.

Moyes, R. (2002) *Addressing the Challenging Behaviour of Children with High-Functioning Autism/Asperger Syndrome in the Classroom – A Guide for Teachers and Parents*. London: Jessica Kingsley Publishers.

Moyes, R.A. (2001) *Incorporating Social Goals in the Classroom: A Guide for Teachers and Parents of Children with High-Functioning Autism and Asperger Syndrome*. London: Jessica Kingsley Publishers.

Nowicki, S. and Duke, M. (1992) *Helping the Child Who Doesn't Fit In*. Atlanta, GA: Peachtree Publishers.

Shure, M. (1995) *Raising a Thinking Child Workbook*. New York: Henry Hold and Company.

Winner, M.G. (2003) *Thinking about You Thinking about Me*. London: Jessica Kingsley Publishers.

Winner, M.G. (2000) *Inside Out: What Makes a Person with Social-cognitive Deficits Tick?* London: Jessica Kingsley Publishers.

Websites

www.ccoder.com/gainingface
Software program to help individuals recognize emotions from facial expressions.

www.graycenter.org
Gray Center for Social Learning and Understanding

www.O.A.S.I.S.
Online Asperger Syndrome information and support.

www.polyxo.com
An introduction to social stories.

TEACCH

www.unc.edu/depts/teach
University of North Carolina, Chapel Hill Teacch Program

Toilet training

Books

Wheeler, M. (1998) *Toilet Training for Individuals with Autism and Related Disorders: A Comprehensive Guide for Parents and Teachers.* Arlington, TX: Future Horizons.

Informational and product websites

ablebaby.com
Able Baby Company offers information and products.

www.frs-inc.com
Autism and Developmental Disabilities Resource Catalogue

www.isn.net/~jypsy/toileting.htm
Oops Wrong Planet syndrome website section on toileting provides a variety of links for more information and resources on toilet training.

www.lee-bee.com
Lee-Bee motivational charts

www.newsignal.com
Hop-On Musical Potty

www.parentsplace.com
The Parents Place is a source of information, recommendations and resources.

www.pppent.com
Positive Parenting Products offers supplies and products.

www.thepottystore.com
The Potty Store offers supplies and products.

www.tinkletoonz.com
Tinkletoonz Potty plays music to offer immediate positive reinforcement.

Tourette's Syndrome

Tourette Syndrome Association
42-40 Bell Blvd
Bayside NY 11361
USA
Phone: 718-224-2999
www.tourette-syndrome.com

Books

Haerle, T. (ed) (1992) *Children with Tourette Syndrome: A Parents' Guide.* Rockville, MD: Woodbine House.

Websites

www.kidsville.net/ts
Tourette Friendship and Support Circle Home Page

www.mentalhealth.com
Internet Mental Health Site

www.tourettesyndrome.net
Tourette Syndrome Plus Home Page

www.tsa-usa.org
Tourette Syndrome Association, Inc

Vaccinations

Websites

www.909shot.com
National Vaccine Information Center (in the US)

www.cdc.gov/nip CDC
national immunization program in the US

www.fda.gov/cber/vaers/vaers.htm
Vaccine Adverse Event Recording System (VAERS)

www.gti.net/truegrit
Autism Autoimmunity Project

www.gval.com
Global Vaccine Awareness League

www.hrsa.dhhs.gov/bhpr/vicp/new.htm
National Vaccine Injury Compensation Program (NVICP)

www.iom.edu
Institute of Medicine

www.nichd.nih.gov/autism
National Institute of Child Health and Human Development

www.vaccineinfo.net
Parents requesting open vaccine education (PROVE)

Vision Therapy

Websites

www.pavevision.org
Parents Active for Vision Education

www.vision-therapy.com
Many links

Vitamins and nutritional supplements

Books

Murray, M. (1996) *Encyclopedia of Nutritional Supplements: The Essential Guide for Improving Your Health Naturally.* New York: Prima Publishing.

Seroussi, K. (2000) *Unraveling the Mystery of Autism and Pervasive Developmental Disorder: A Mother's Story of Research and Recovery.* New York: Simon & Schuster.

Websites

www.autism.com/ari
Autism Research Institute

www.eas.asu.edu/~autism
For specific types of vitamins/minerals and recommended dosages recommended by James Adams, Ph.D. and Woody McGinnis, M.D.

www.megson.com
Dr Mary Megson's site with information on Vitamin A and Autism.

www.nutrition.gov
The United States RDA official government reports on the new Adequate Intake (AI) to prevent disease.

Resources created and run by parents

Books by parents

Fling, E. (2000) *Eating an Artichoke: A Mother's Perspective on Asperger Syndrome.* London: Jessica Kingsley Publishers.

Hamilton, L.M. (2000) *Facing Autism: Giving Parents Reasons for Hope and Guidance for Help.* Colorado Springs, CO: Waterbrook Press.

Hughes, R. (2003) *Running with Walker: A Memoir.* London: Jessica Kingsley Publishers.

Kephart, B. (1998) *A Slant of Sun: One Child's Courage*. New York: W.W. Norton.

Paradiz, V. (2002) *Elijah's Cup: A Family's Journey into the Community and Culture of High-functioning Autism and Asperger's Syndrome*. New York: Free Press.

Seroussi, K. (2000) *Unraveling the Mystery of Autism and Pervasive Developmental Disorder: A Mother's Story of Research and Recovery*. New York: Simon & Schuster.

Websites

www.angelfire.com/ky/tourisinfor/tempertantrum.htm
Written by a mother describing her personal experience in dealing with temper tantrums.

www.autisminfo.com
Created by Brad and Jenny Middlebrook with daily updates on many areas of information on ASD.

www.autism-spectrum.com
Information, news, chat rooms, book reviews...

www.trainland.tripod.com
Created by Kay Stammers for parents just starting out and needing to get beyond the ASD label.

wmoore.net/therapy.html
Listings of summer camps for children with special needs in the US, Canada and Mexico.

Sites for physicians

allergyconnection.com
Site authored by Dr Richard Layton (pediatric and allergy specialist).

www.amug.org/~a203table_contents.html
Asperger/Autism: On the Same Page

home.san.rr.com/autismnet
Autism Network Resources for Physicians

www.lifestages.comheathl/autsim/html
The Autism File – described as a Cliff Notes (brief synopsis) on
Autism research by Autism Digest Magazine.

Resources just for kids
Books

Amenta, C.A. (1992) *Russell is Extra Special: A Book about Autism for Children.* New York: Magination Press.

Carlson, R. Jr. (2002) *My brother Kevin has Autism.* Lincoln, NE: Writers Club Press.

Carlson, R. Jr. (2002) *Poems and Short Stories About my Brother Kevin who has Autism.* Lincoln, NE: Writers Club Press.

Hoopmann, K. (2003) *Haze: An Asperger Novel.* London: Jessica Kingsley Publishers.

Hoopmann, K. (2002) *Lisa and the Lacemaker.* London: Jessica Kingsley Publishers.

Hoopmann, K. (2001) *Of Mice and Aliens an Asperger Adventure.* London: Jessica Kingsley Publishers.

Hoopmann, K. (1998) *Blue Bottle Mystery: An Asperger Adventure.* London: Jessica Kingsley Publishers.

Messner, A.W. and Belliveau, K. (1996) *Captain Tommy: A Story Designed to Help Children Understand Their Peers with Autism.* Arlington, TX: Future Horizons.

Ogaz, N. (2002) *Buster and the Amazing Daisy.* London: Jessica Kingsley Publishers.

Sainsbury, C. (2000) *Martian in the Playground.* Bristol: Lucky Duck Publishing.

Websites

www.cdc.gov/ncbddd/kids/kautismpage.htm
Centres for Disease Control and Prevention's (CDC) site on
information about autism written for kids.

www.kidspsych.org
KidsPsych has game sections for kids and information for parents.

Resources about or developed by individuals diagnosed with ASD

Books

Grandin, T. (1996) *Emergence: Labelled Autistic.* New York: Warner.

Grandin, T. (1996) *Thinking in Pictures.* New York: Vintage Books.

Hall, K. (2000) *Asperger Syndrome, the University and Everything.* London: Jessica Kingsley Publishers.

Holliday Willey, L. (2001) *Asperger Syndrome in the Family: Redefining Normal.* London: Jessica Kingsley Publishers.

Holliday Willey, L (1999) *Pretending to be Normal.* London: Jessica Kingsley Publishers.

Jackson, L. (2002) *Freaks, Geeks and Asperger Syndrome.* London: Jessica Kingsley Publishers.

Lawson, W. (2003) *Build your own Life – A Self-help Guide For Individuals with Asperger Syndrome.* London: Jessica Kingsley Publishers.

Lawson, W. (2001) *Understanding and Working with the Spectrum of Autism: An Insider's View.* London: Jessica Kingsley Publishers.

Lawson, W. (1998) *Life Behind Glass.* Lismore, NSW: Southern Cross Univeristy Press and (2000) London: Jessica Kingsley Publishers.

O'Neill, J.L. (1998) *Through the Eyes of Aliens: A Book about Autistic People.* London: Jessica Kingsley Publishers.

Williams, D. (1998) *Autism and Sensing: The Unlost Instinct.* London: Jessica Kingsley Publishers.

Williams, D. (1998) *Like Colour to the Blind – Soul Searching and Soul Finding.* London: Jessica Kingsley Publishers.

Williams, D. (1994) *Somebody Somewhere.* London: Jessica Kingsley Publishers.

Williams, D. (1992) *Nobody Nowhere.* London: Jessica Kingsley Publishers.

Websites

www.hugsfeelgood.com/kevincarlson.html
Kevin Carlson, an autistic Savant, is an illustrator of children's books.

82 What websites are available to provide therapy tools, learning activities and materials for working with ASD individuals?

www.aacintervention.com
Caroline Musselwhite's shared site.

www.attainment.com
Attainment Company (communication displays)

www.babybumblebee.com
Language development with videos and CDs.

www.creative-comm.com
Pati King deBaun's company website.

www.donjohnston.com
Learning Intervention Resources.

www.do2learn.com
Provides learning activities, free printable material.

www.enablingdevices.com
Toys for special children.

www.frame-tech.com
Communication devices that are affordable and innovative.

www.hiphopraplyrics.com
Lyrics that can be used with older students.

www.hyperstudio.com
Hyperstudio Multi-media software.

www.intellitools.com
IntelliTools company (IntelliKeys)

www.kidspsych.org
Games for children aged 1–9 with a section on Information for Parents.

www.LaureateLearning.com
A product site for language intervention software.

www.lburkhart.com
Linda Burkhart's resource site (AAC).

www.lyrics.natalnet.com.br/html/main-index/
Song lyrics.

www.magicaltoysandproducts.com
Products to promote sensory awareness.

www.mayer-johnson.com
Mayer Johnson Company (Boardmaker, PCS libraries)

www.readplease.com
Text to speech application.

www.sfaw.com
An open book initiative with reading resource links.

www.smartkidssoftware.com
Software for children.

www.spectronicsinoz.com/browse.asp?cat=10
Spectronic Inclusive Learning Technologies – books and resources in Australia.

www.stageslearning.com
Product site for photographic flash cards.

www.switchintime.com
Accessible switch software titles.

www.thegateway.org
Educational resources on the web.

www.therapyfun4kids.com
Creative and affordable therapy toys and supplies.

www.tinsnips.com
For pre-kindergarten and kindergarten age children.

www.widgit.com
Widgit Software

Diagnostic Criteria for Autism

DSM-IV Diagnostic Criteria for 299.00 Autistic Disorder (DSM-IV, APA, 1994)

A.   A total of six (or more) items from (1), (2), and (3), with at least two from (1), and one each from (2) and (3).

  (1)   qualitative impairment in social interaction, as manifested by at least two of the following:

   a.   marked impairment in the use of multiple nonverbal behaviors such as eye-to-eye gaze, facial expression, body postures and gestures to regulate social interaction

 ? b.   failure to develop peer relationships appropriate to developmental level

   c.   a lack of spontaneous seeking to share enjoyment, interests, or achievements with other people (e.g., by a lack of showing, bringing, or pointing out objects of interest)

   d.   lack of social or emotional reciprocity

  (2)   qualitative impairments in communication as manifested by at least one of the following:

   a.   delay in, or total lack of, the development of spoken language (not accompanied by an attempt to compensate through alternative

modes of communication such as gesture or
mime)

(b.) in individuals with adequate speech, marked
impairment in the ability to initiate or sustain a
conversation with others

c. stereotyped and repetitive use of language or
idiosyncratic language

d. lack of varied, spontaneous make-believe play or
social imitative play appropriate to
developmental level

(3) restricted repetitive and stereotyped patterns of
behavior, interests, and activities, as manifested by at
least one of the following:

a. encompassing preoccupation with one or more
stereotyped and restricted patterns of interest
that is abnormal either in intensity or focus

b. apparently inflexible adherence to specific,
nonfunctional routines or rituals

c. stereotyped and repetitive motor mannerisms
(e.g., hand or finger flapping or twisting, or
complex whole-body movement)

d. persistent preoccupation with parts of objects

B. Delays or abnormal functioning in at least one of the
following areas, with onset prior to age 3 years: (1) social
interaction, (2) language as used in social communication,
or (3) symbolic or imaginative play.

C. The disturbance is not better accounted for by Rett's
Disorder or Childhood Disintegrative Disorder.

Source: (1994) *Diagnostic and Statistical Manual of Mental Disorders* (4th edn)
Washington, DC: American Psychiatric Association. pp.70, 71.

Diagnostic Criteria For Autism (ICD-10, WHO, 1992)

F84.0 Childhood Autism

A type of pervasive developmental disorder that is defined by: (a) the presence of abnormal or impaired development that is manifest before the age of three years, and (b) the characteristic type of abnormal functioning in all the three areas of psychopathology: reciprocal social interaction, communication, and restricted, stereotyped, repetitive behaviour. In addition to these specific diagnostic features, a range of other nonspecific problems are common, such as phobias, sleeping and eating disturbances, temper tantrums, and (self-directed) aggression.

F84.1 Atypical Autism

A type of pervasive developmental disorder that differs from childhood autism either in age of onset or in failing to fulfil all three sets of diagnostic criteria. This subcategory should be used when there is abnormal and impaired development that is present only after age three years; and a lack of sufficient demonstrable abnormalities in one or two of the three areas of psychopathology required for the diagnosis of autism (namely, reciprocal social interactions, communication, and restrictive, stereotyped, repetitive behaviour) in spite of characteristic abnormalities in the other area(s). Atypical autism arises most often in profoundly retarded individuals and in individuals with a severe specific developmental disorder of receptive language.

Source: (1992) *International Statistical Classification of Diseases and Related Health Problems* (10th revision). Geneva, Switzerland: World Health Organization. p.376.

Diagnostic Criteria for Asperger's Disorder

Diagnostic Criteria for 299.00 Asperger's Disorder (DSM-IV, APA 1994)

A. Qualitative impairment in social interaction, as manifested by at least two of the following:

  ? 1) marked impairment in the use of multiple nonverbal behaviors such as eye-to-eye gaze, facial expression, body postures, and gestures to regulate social interaction

  2) failure to develop peer relationships appropriate to developmental level

  3) a lack of spontaneous seeking to share enjoyment, interests or achievements with other people (e.g.: by a lack of showing, bringing, or pointing out objects of interest to other people)

  4) lack of social or emotional reciprocity

B. Restricted repetitive and stereotyped patterns of behavior, interests, and activities, as manifested by at least one of the following:

  1) encompassing preoccupation with one or more stereotyped and restricted patterns of interest that is abnormal either in intensity or focus

2)   apparently inflexible adherence to specific, nonfunctional routine or rituals

3)   stereotyped and repetitive motor mannerisms (e.g: hand or finger flapping or twisting, or complex whole-body movements)

4)   persistent preoccupation with parts of objects

C.   The disturbance causes clinically significant impairment in social, occupational, or other important areas of functioning.

D.   There is no clinically significant general delay in language (e.g: single words used by age 2 years, communicative phrases used by age 3 years).

E.   There is no clinically significant delay in cognitive development or in the development of age-appropriate self-help skills, adaptive behavior (other than social interaction), and curiosity about the environment in childhood.

F.   Criteria are not met for another specific Pervasive Developmental Disorder, or Schizophrenia.

Source: (1994) *Diagnostic and Statistical Manual of Mental Disorders* (4th edn). Washington, DC: American Psychiatric Association. p.77.

Diagnostic Criteria for Asperger's Disorder (ICD-10, WHO, 1992)

F84.5 Asperger's Syndrome

A disorder of uncertain nosological validity, characterized by the same type of qualitative abnormalities of reciprocal social interaction that typify autism, together with a restricted, stereotyped, repetitive repertoire of interests and activities. It differs from autism primarily in the fact that there is no general delay or retardation in language or in cognitive development. This disorder is often associated with marked clumsiness. There is a strong tendency for the abnormalities to persist into adolescence and adult life. Psychotic episodes occasionally occur in early adult life.

Source: (1992) *International Statistical Classification of Diseases and Related Health Problems* (10th revision). Geneva, Switxerland: World Health Organization. p.377.

Diagnostic Criteria for Rett's Disorder (DSM-IV, ICD-10 and Rett Syndrome Association)

Diagnostic Criteria for 299.80 Rett's Disorder (DSM-IV, APA, 1994)

A.   All of the following:

   (1)   apparently normal prenatal and perinatal development

   (2)   apparently normal psychomotor development through the first 5 months after birth

   (3)   normal head circumference at birth

B.   Onset of all of the following after the period of normal development

   (1)   deceleration of head growth between ages 5 and 48 months

   (2)   loss of previously acquired purposeful hand skills between ages 5 and 30 months with the subsequent development of stereotyped hand movements (e.g., hand-wringing or hand washing)

   (3)   loss of social engagement early in the course (although often social interaction develops later)

(4)   appearance of poorly coordinated gait or trunk
movements

(5)   severely impaired expressive and receptive language
development with severe psychomotor retardation

Source: (1994) *Diagnostic and Statistical Manual of Mental Disorders* (4th edn). Washington, DC: American Psychiatric Association. pp.72, 73.

NOTE: In September 2001 the International Rett Syndrome Association (IRSA) developed a revised set of criteria for the diagnosis of Rett Syndrome subsequent to the knowledge base and discovery of the MECP2 gene. Although the essential components of those criteria listed above remained, there was some clarification in the language used to reduce the ambiguity. The necessary diagnostic criteria for Rett Syndrome according to the IRSA are:

1.   apparently normal prenatal and perinatal history

2.   psychomotor development largely normal through the first six months or may be delayed from birth

3.   normal head circumference at birth

4.   postnatal deceleration of head growth in the majority

5.   loss of achieved purposeful hand skill between ages ½ to 2 and ½ years

6.   stereotypic hand movements such as hand wringing/squeezing, clapping/tapping, mouthing and washing/rubbing automatisms

7.   emerging social withdrawal, communication dysfunction, loss of learning words, and cognitive impairment

8.   impaired (dyspraxic) or failing locomotion

Criteria source: www.rettsyndrome.org

Diagnostic Critera for Rett's Disorder (ICD-10, WHO 1992)

F84.2 Rett's syndrome

A condition, so far found only in girls, in which apparently normal early development is followed by partial or complete loss of speech and of skills in locomotion and use of hands, together with deceleration in head growth, usually with an onset of between 7 and 24 months of age. Loss of purposive hand movements, hand wringing stereotypes and hyperventilation are characteristic. Social play and development are arrested but social interest tends to be maintained. Trunk ataxia and apraxia start to develop by age four years and choreoathetoid momements frequently follow. Severe mental retardation almost invariably results.

Source: (1992) *International Statistical Classification of Diseases and Related Health Problems* (10th revision). Geneva, Switzerland: World Health Organization. p.376.

APPENDIX D

Diagnostic Criteria for Childhood Disintegrative Disorder

Diagnostic Criteria for 299.10 Childhood Disintegrative Disorder (DSM-IV, APA, 1994)

A. Apparently normal development for at least the first 2 years after birth as manifested by the presence of age-appropriate verbal and nonverbal communication, social relationships, play and adaptive behavior.

B. Clinically significant loss of previously acquired skills (before the age of 10 years) in at least two of the following areas:

    (1)   expressive or receptive language

    (2)   social skills or adaptive behavior

    (3)   bowel or bladder control

    (4)   play

    (5)   motor skills

C. Abnormalities of functioning in at least two of the following areas:

    (1)   qualitative impairment in social interaction (e.g., impairment in nonverbal behaviors, failure to develop peer relationships, lack of social or emotional reciprocity)

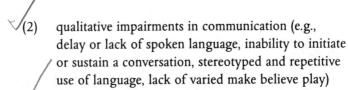

(2)   qualitative impairments in communication (e.g., delay or lack of spoken language, inability to initiate or sustain a conversation, stereotyped and repetitive use of language, lack of varied make believe play)

(3)   restricted, repetitive, and stereotyped patterns of behavior, interests, and activities, including motor stereotypies and mannerisms.

D.   The disturbance is not better accounted for by another specific Pervasive Developmental Disorder or by Schizophrenia

Source: (1994) *Diagnostic and Statistical Manual of Mental Disorders* (4th edn). Washington, DC: American Psychiatric Association. pp.74, 75.

Diagnostic Criteria for Other Childhood Disintegrative Disorder (ICD-10, WHO 1992)

F84.3 Other childhood disintergrative disorder

A type of pervasive developmental disorder that is defined by a period of entirely normal development before the onset of the disorder, followed by a definite loss of previously acquired skills in several areas accompanied by a general loss of interest in the environment, by stereotyped, repetitive motor mannerism, and by autistic-like abnormalities in social interaction and communication. In some cases the disorder can be shown to be due to some associated encephalopathy but the diagnosis should be made on the behavioral features.

Source: (1992) *International Statistical Classification of Diseases and Related Health Problems* (10th revision). Geneva, Switzerland: World Health Organization. p.377.

Test Instruments

Asperger Syndrome Diagnostic Scale (ASDS)
Authors: Brenda Smith Myles, Stacy Jones-Bock and Richard L. Simpson (2000)

Purpose: To quickly identify Asperger Syndrome in children aged 5–18 through a rating scale of 50 yes/no items. An AS Quotient measures the likelihood that an individual has Asperger Syndrome.

Autism Behavior Checklist (ABC)
Authors: David A. Krug, Joel R. Arick and Patricia J. Almond (1978)

Purpose: A screening instrument to identify nonadaptive behaviors by circling which items best represent the behaviors of an individual. Part of the ASIEP-2 described below although it can be administered independent of other subtests.

Autism Diagnostic Interview–Revised (ADI-R)
Authors: Ann LeCouteur M.D., Catherine Lord Ph.D. and Michael Rutter M.D. (2003)

Purpose: This tool is a comprehensive interview that was widely used in research and is expected to be available for clinical use in the summer of 2003.

Autism Diagnostic Observation Schedule–Generic (ADOS-G)
Authors: C. Lord, M. Rutter, R. DiLavore, S. Risis (1999)

Purpose: To assess children and adults of various developmental and language levels pertaining to communication, social interaction and play skills. This instrument is a combination of the Autism Diagnostic Observation Schedule (ADOS) and the Pre-Linguistic Autism Diagnostic Observation Scale (PL-ADOS).

Autism Research Institute (ARI) Form E-2: Diagnostic Checklist
Authors: Autism Research Institute, Bernard Rimland (1971)

Purpose: Diagnostic checklist and research questionnaire used by the Autism Research Institute for gathering data and providing the individual submitting the form with a score and interpretation of its meaning.

Autism Screening Instrument for Educational Planning (ASIEP-2)
Authors: David A. Krug, Joel R. Arick and Patricia J. Almond (1993)

Purpose: Five different scales evaluate an individual's functional abilities and instructional needs. Percentile and summary scores are available for individual subtests.

Behavior Rating Instrument for Autistic and Other Atypical Children (BRIAAC)
Authors: Bertram A. Ruttenberg MD, Charles Wenar PhD and Enid G. Wolf EdD (1991)

Purpose: To evaluate the status of low-functioning, atypical or Autistic children using seven scales of observing behavior.

Checklist for Autism in Toddlers (CHAT)
Authors: Simon Baron-Cohen *et al.* (1992)

Purpose: To assist health care professionals during an 18-month-old developmental check-up in identifying children who are at risk for social-communication disorders.

Childhood Autism Rating Scale (CARS)
Authors: Eric Schopler, Robert L. Reichler and Barbara Rochen Renner (1988)

Purpose: A rating scale that allows the examiner to distinguish mild to moderate from severe Autism in five different areas. Appropriate for use with anyone over the age of 2.

Developmental Behaviour Checklist (DBC) Early Screen
Author: Kylie Gray (2002)

Purpose: To identify Autism in children as young as 18 months in order to make appropriate referrals for early diagnostic assessments and intervention.

Gilliam Asperger's Disorder Scale (GADS)
Author: James E. Gilliam (2000)

Purpose: To distinguish individuals with Asperger's Syndrome from other related pervasive developmental disorders in individuals between 3 and 22 years of age.

Gilliam Autism Rating Scale (GARS)
Author: James E. Gilliam (1995)

Purpose: Used to identify and diagnose Autism and to estimate the severity of the disorder in individuals between the ages of 3 and 22.

Pervasive Developmental Disorders Screening Test (PDDST-II)
Author: Bryna Siegel (1996)

Purpose: This test is designed to help health care professionals obtain information from parents via a questionnaire in order to determine whether a child should be evaluated for ASD.

The Australian Scale for Asperger's Syndrome
Authors: Michelle S. Garnett and Anthony J. Attwood (2nd edn, 1994)

Purpose: A questionnaire designed to identify behaviors and abilities of primary school age children that are consistent with a diagnosis of Asperger's Syndrome.

The Modified Checklist for Autism in Toddlers (M-CHAT)
Authors: Diane L. Robins M.A., Deborah Fein Ph.D., Marianne L. Barton Ph.D. and James A. Green Ph.D. (2001)

Purpose: To differentiate individuals with ASD from normally developing children in order to make appropriate referrals for a more comprehensive assessment of ASD. It is a revised and expanded version of the original CHAT developed in the United Kingdom.

Medications

The medications indicated below are currently being used to address various symptoms associated with ASD. However, efficacy for use of these drugs in children with ASD is limited. The Children's Medication Chart below indicates ages for approved drug usage. There are new studies being conducted and new medications currently being developed. In fact, Prozac was approved for children between 7 and 17 at the time of writing but after the research that was used to provide the medication chart below.

Medications should always be taken under the guidance of a physician and instructions should be followed exactly. Be sure to inform the physician of all products being taken including vitamins, minerals, supplements, enzymes, etc when considering any medication. Even "natural" alternatives can have side effects or cause negative reactions when taken with prescribed medication. This appendix is for information purposes only and it is not intended to be medical advice.

Alphabetical List of Medications
by Generic Name

GENERIC NAME	TRADE NAME
Antipsychotic Medications	
chlorpromazine	Thorazine
chlorprothixene	Taractan
clozapine	Clozaril
fluphenazine	Permitil, Prolixin
haloperidol	Haldol
loxapine	Loxitane
mesoridazine	Serentil
molindone	Lidone, Moban
olanzapine	Zyprexa
perphenazine	Trilafon
pimozide (for Tourette's Syndrome)	Orap
quetiapine	Seroquel
risperidone	Risperdal
thioridazine	Mellaril
thiothixene	Navane
trifluoperazine	Stelazine
trifluopromazine	Vesprin
ziprasidone	Geodon

Antimanic Medications

carbamazepine	Tegretol
divalproex sodium (valproic acid)	Depakote
gabapentin	Neurontin
lamotrigine	Lamictal
topimarate	Topamax
lithium carbonate	Eskalith, Lithane, Lithobid
lithium citrate	Cibalith-S

Antidepressant Medications

amitriptyline	Elavil
amoxapine	Asendin
bupropion	Wellbutrin
citalopram (SSRI)	Celexa
clomipramine	Anafranil
desipramine	Norpramin, Pertofrane
doxepin	Adapin, Sinequan
fluvoxamine (SSRI)	Luvox
fluoxetine (SSRI)	Prozac
imipramine	Tofranil
isocarboxazid (MAOI)	Marplan
maprotiline	Ludiomil
mirtazapine	Remeron
nefazodone	Serzone
nortriptyline	Aventyl, Pamelor

paroxetine (SSRI)	Paxil
phenelzine (MAOI)	Nardil
protriptyline	Vivactil
sertraline (SSRI)	Zoloft
tranylcypromine (MAOI)	Parnate
trazodone	Desyrel
trimipramine	Surmontil
venlafaxine	Effexor

Antianxiety Medications

(All of these antianxiety medications except buspirone are benzodiazepines)

alprazolam	Xanax
buspirone	BuSpar
chlordiazepoxide	Librax, Libritabs, Librium
clonazepam	Klonopin
clorazepate	Azene, Tranxene
diazepam	Valium
halazepam	Paxipam
lorazepam	Ativan
oxazepam	Serax
prazepam	Centrax

Alphabetical List of Medications
by Trade Name

TRADE NAME	GENERIC NAME
Antipsychotic Medications	
Clozaril	clozapine
Geodon	ziprasidone
Haldol	haloperidol
Lidone	molindone
Loxitane	loxapine
Mellaril	thioridazine
Moban	molindone
Navane	thiothixene
Orap (for Tourette's Syndrome)	pimozide
Permitil	fluphenazine
Prolixin	fluphenazine
Risperdal	risperidone
Serentil	mesoridazine
Seroquel	quetiapine
Stelazine	trifluoperazine
Taractan	chlorprothixene
Thorazine	chlorpromazine
Trilafon	perphenazine
Vesprin	trifluopromazine
Zyprexa	olanzapine

Antimanic Medications	
Cibalith-S	lithium citrate
Depakote	valproic acid, divalproex sodium
Eskalith	lithium carbonate
Lamictal	lamotrigine
Lithane	lithium carbonate
Lithobid	lithium carbonate
Neurontin	gabapentin
Tegretol	carbamazepine
Topamax	topiramate
Antidepressant Medications	
Adapin	doxepin
Anafranil	clomipramine
Asendin	amoxapine
Aventyl	nortriptyline
Celexa (SSRI)	citalopram
Desyrel	trazodone
Effexor	venlafaxine
Elavil	amitriptyline
Ludiomil	maprotiline
Luvox (SSRI)	fluvoxamine
Marplan (MAOI)	isocarboxazid
Nardil (MAOI)	phenelzine
Norpramin	desipramine
Pamelor	nortriptyline

Parnate (MAOI)	tranylcypromine
Paxil (SSRI)	paroxetine
Pertofrane	desipramine
Prozac (SSRI)	fluoxetine
Remeron	mirtazapine
Serzone	nefazodone
Sinequan	doxepin
Surmontil	trimipramine
Tofranil	imipramine
Vivactil	protriptyline
Wellbutrin	bupropion
Zoloft (SSRI)	sertraline

Antianxiety Medications

(All of these antianxiety medications except BuSpar are benzodiazepines)

Ativan	lorazepam
Azene	clorazepate
BuSpar	buspirone
Centrax	prazepam
Klonopin	clonazepam
Librax, Libritabs, Librium	chlordiazepoxide
Paxipam	halazepam
Serax	oxazepam
Tranxene	clorazepate
Valium	diazepam
Xanax	alprazolam

Children's Medication Chart

TRADE NAME	GENERIC NAME	APPROVED AGE
Stimulant Medications		
Adderall	amphetamine	3 and older
Adderall XR	amphetamine (extended release)	6 and older
Concerta	methylphenidate (long acting)	6 and older
Cylert*	pemoline	6 and older
Dexedrine	dextroamphetamine	3 and older
Dextrostat	dextroamphetamine	3 and older
Focalin	dexmenthylphenidate	6 and older
Metadate ER	methylphenidate (extended release)	6 and older
Ritalin	methylphenidate	6 and older

*Because of its potential for serious side effects affecting the liver, Cylert should not ordinarily be considered as first-line drug therapy for ADHD.

Antidepressant and Antianxiety Medications		
Anafranil	clomipramine	10 and older (for OCD)
BuSpar	buspirone	18 and older
Effexor	venlafaxine	18 and older
Luvox (SSRI)	fluvoxamine	8 and older (for OCD)
Paxil (SSRI)	paroxetine	18 and older
Prozac (SSRI)	fluoxetine	7 and older *
Serzone (SSRI)	nefazodone	18 and older
Sinequan	doxepin	12 and older
Tofranil	imipramine	6 and older (for bedwetting)
Wellbutrin	bupropion	18 and older
Zoloft (SSRI)	sertraline	6 and older (for OCD)

* Information not in original source: Prozac usage for children 7 to 17 just approved by the US Food and Drug Administration (FDA) for depression and OCD in children.

Mood Stabilizing Medications		
Cibalith-S	lithium citrate	12 and older
Depakote	valproic acid	2 and older (for seizures)
Eskalith	lithium carbonate	12 and older
Lithobid	lithium carbonate	12 and older
Tegretol	carbamazepine	any age (for seizures)

Antipsychotic Medications		
Clozaril (atypical)	clozapine	18 and older
Haldol	haloperidol	3 and older
Risperdal (atypical)	risperidone	18 and older
Seroquel (atypical)	quetiapine	18 and older
Mellaril	thioridazine	2 and older
Zyprexa (atypical)	olanzapine	18 and older
Orap	pimozide	12 and older (for Tourette's Syndrome – data for age 2 and older indicate similar safety profile)

Sources:

Physicians' Desk Reference, 54th edition (2000) Montavale, NJ: Medical Economics Data Production Co.

Medications, 4th edition (2002) Bethesda, MD: The National Institute of Mental Health. NIH Publication No.02-3929.